SPAIN

an amazingly short history

by
BOB FOWKE

Travelbrief Publications

Published in 2004 by Travelbrief Publications

0-9548351-0-7

10 9 8 7 6 5 4 3 2 1

Travelbrief Publications
7 Brougham Square, Shrewsbury SY3 7PE

Printed and bound by Cambrian Printers, Aberystwyth, UK

CONTENTS

Acknowledgement
With thanks to Andrew Mee and Robert Branton. Their help with the writing of this book has been invaluable.

INTRODUCTION
WHO TO PRUNE?
- AND WHY TO PRUNE THEM

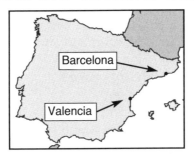

Hola!

The motorway south from Barcelona to Valencia snakes between citrus orchards, vineyards and almond groves. To the left, coastal resorts hug the shore, their backs towards you. To the right, the foothills of central Spain rise skywards. The motorway is new - and fast. Distant spots in the rear-view mirror swell into impatient gas-guzzlers on the back bumper, swoosh past and disappear into the southern haze, all in a minute.

This coastal strip has been much fought over. Here, Romans bashed the natives into submission, El Cid performed deeds of derring-do, Muslims and Christians slugged it out for supremacy and, more recently, Nationalists and Republicans took their bitter quarrel to its murderous conclusion.

Spain is a country with an incredibly rich past. There's hardly a square metre of land which doesn't have some story to tell if we only knew what it was, or if we had the time to find out.

Here is the story of that land - the short version. The

5

complete version would describe literally thousands of bloody battles, and hundreds of thousands of passionate love affairs, betrayals, deeds of kindness and acts of cruelty - the actions of millions of individuals over a vast number of years. Thousands of these long-gone individuals were important to the story of Spain and hundreds of them were absolutely indispensable.

Most have been ruthlessly pruned.

Forgive the poor writer who had to decide who to prune and who to leave standing, which battles to describe and which to ignore, which artists, scientists, writers, handsome courtiers and beautiful women should be consigned to the dustbin and which should be retained for at least a mention.

Bob Fowke August 2004

1492

FROM GRANADA TO AMERICA

Columbus and the pretty queen

It was the winter of 1491. The city of Granada was under siege by the rulers of the kingdoms of Castile and Aragón to the north. On level ground not far from the city walls, the besiegers had built a large, military camp. The siege had gone

on so long that this camp had grown into a small town, a forest of tents, makeshift buildings and fluttering flags. It had a church, a drill ground and even a temporary, one-storey palace in the centre for the king and queen who led the siege. From the palace windows they could gaze on the Alhambra, fortress of the Muslim rulers of Granada, rising beautiful and battered above the starving city.

In the temporary palace a meeting was taking place, a difficult meeting. On one side, the most powerful woman in Spain, the most Christian Queen Isabella of Castile, on the other side, Christopher Columbus, the soon-to-be discoverer of America. Columbus was a tall man with blue eyes, attractive to women; Isabella was a small, slightly plump woman with a pretty face. At their first meeting six years earlier, he'd charmed her into believing in his madcap scheme for a voyage *west* to China and the Indies, on the widely-accepted belief that the world was round. Now she'd decided to back him, even though he was a nobody, a poor Italian adventurer. She'd even sent him a purse of money before their meeting, just so he could buy himself a decent suit of clothes.

If you're in Granada
Ferdinand and Isabella's temporary palace at Santa Fé, their military camp outside Granada, has been restored and is open to visitors.

Columbus had planned for this meeting for years, so why was he being so obnoxious now? He strutted, he argued. Before he 'agreed' to go, he wanted a noble title, the rank of Grand Admiral and near-absolute powers over all the lands which he might discover. Plus ten percent commission on all trade between any newly-discovered lands and Spain.

Columbus's demands were outrageous. Isabella broke off the meeting to consult with her husband, King Ferdinand. They were both clear: Columbus must reduce his price or else the deal was off. Columbus refused. He left the palace in a huff and rode out of Santa Fé, through the defensive walls and over the massive moat which had been hastily dug around them. All he took with him was 'the night and day' - a Spanish idiom meaning 'nothing at all' - and his pride.

But then, in one of those moments of history which change the world, Isabella had second thoughts. Her advisers pointed out that this tall, irritating Italian was by far the best man to lead such an important voyage of discovery. It was Columbus's project from start to finish. She was reminded that it would cost her nothing to award him a noble title and the rank of Grand Admiral. As for the ten percent commission - if he discovered vast new lands, he'd be worth every penny of it. She changed her mind. A court official was sent out on a good, fast horse. Since Columbus was riding an old nag, it didn't take long to catch him up.

Soon after that, they signed a contract. Columbus was appointed leader of an expedition to discover the Indies via a western route. And soon after *that* came the new year.

And with the new year came 1492 - the most important year in Spanish history.

* In 1492, Isabella and Ferdinand captured Granada from the Muslims, thus ending a seven-hundred year Christian campaign to reconquer Muslim Spain.
* In 1492, Isabella and Ferdinand threw out the Jews, causing great suffering.
* In 1492 Columbus discovered America, winning a vast empire for the Spanish crown.

From being an isolated, war-torn country on the fringes of Europe, Spain became a world super-power almost overnight. It's because of 1492 that Spanish language and culture dominate vast areas of the modern world.

To find out how Spain got to 1492, and why it's called 'Spain' at all, we have to go back a very long way ...

Why 'Spain'

and: *do rabbits speak Spanish?*

Add facial expression, and the map of Spain and Portugal resembles a creature sniffing at the coast of Morocco.

The Pyrenees are the collar of this creature, a collar with large, snow-capped studs on it. They're big mountains. They divide Spain from Europe almost as effectively as the English Channel divides Europe from Britain. Like the Channel, they've formed a barrier against foreign armies and foreign influences from time immemorial. They've allowed Spain to develop its fabulous, unique culture in semi-isolation.

1. Long, long ago, in the very remote past, this isolated corner of Europe was called *Iberia*. *Iber* may have meant 'river' in the language of the ancient Iberians who once lived there. The Iberians may have come from North Africa originally, which is dry. *Iberia* was called after its rivers - its distinguishing feature from the point of view of the newcomers.

Iberia is now the name of the whole peninsula, including Portugal.

2. Around 600 BC, ancient Greeks set up trading posts and small cities along the east Iberian coast. Their name for the land was *Hesperia* which meant 'Land of the Setting Sun' in ancient Greek. To them of course, Spain was in the west.

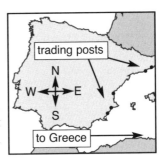

3. Three hundred years after the Greeks arrived, traders from Carthage in North Africa took over a chunk of the southwest. One theory says that, at that time, the land was infested by a large numbers of rabbits and the Carthaginians called it *Ispania*, meaning 'Land of Rabbits', from *sphan* which was their word for rabbit.

4. Finally, along came the Romans. They ignored the setting sun and the rivers and plumped for the rabbits - according to the rabbit theorists. In which case, they based their name on the Carthaginian word *Ispania*, changing it to *Hispania* or *España as* it's called in modern Spanish - 'Spain' in English. The Spanish language, meanwhile, grew out of Latin as spoken by the Romans.

- which is not to say that 'Spanish' means 'rabbit like'. That would be unfair to one of the world's greatest languages.

Spanish History

1973 +	Modern times
1939-73	Dictatorship of General Franco
1936-39	Civil War
1931-36	Second Republic
1808-14	War of Independence
1600-1800	long decline
1492	America discovered, Spanish Empire begins
710-1492	Islamic Spain (and the *Reconquista*)
409-710	Rule by the Visigoths
218 BC - AD 409	Roman Spain
237 BC	Carthaginians arrive
from 600 BC	Ancient Greek colonies
from 1200 BC	Phoenician colonies
from 5-4000 BC	Iberians
peaking 15,000 BC	Stone Age cultures

EARLY SPAIN
BASIC INGREDIENTS

The huntsman of Altamira

One hot afternoon over seventeen thousand years ago, a primitive tribesman clambered deep into a cave in northern Spain. Inside the cave it was relatively cool. Hopefully no lions or other dangerous beasts had taken shelter there. He took an oil lamp with him, earth pigments, water and a brush. Once in the innermost cavern he lay down on his back and sketched the outline of a bison on the low ceiling. Then he began to work into the detail, adding contours and highlights. His only light was the feeble oil lamp, but the lines he drew were swift and sure. Finally, next to the bison, he drew the figure of a man holding a bow, a man like himself.

In actual fact, the artist may have worked at night or may have been a woman, but the figure he or she drew on the cave wall is one of the oldest images of a human being in Spain - the question of who drew him and why inevitably leads one to wonder.

Like hundreds of other paintings in the caves of Altamira, the archer is beautifully done. The man or woman who painted him was a true artist, even though he or she lived such a long time ago. There were many other such artists, their work miraculously preserved at Altamira and other important sites. Spain is littered with evidence of Stone Age Man.

If you're near Santander

The caves of Altamira are hidden beneath a hill close to the medieval village of Santillana del Mar, forty-eight kilometres from Santander on the north coast.

They were discovered in 1868. At that time, the colours of the paintings glowed almost as fresh as if they'd just been painted. Since then, they have been damaged by moisture from the breath of millions of visitors. Now only twenty people per day are allowed inside and only with special permission.

However, you can get a very good idea of what the caves are like in the nearby replica caves at the Museo de Altamira. There are even earlier prehistoric paintings in the caves at Puente Viesgo quite close by, off the N623 Santander/Burgos road.

Cádiz - the oldest city in Europe?

The cave culture of Altamira peaked around 15,000 BC. After that Spain stagnated for many thousands of years - until between 5,000 and 4,000 BC, when the Iberians arrived from North Africa and called it *Iberia*. The Iberians were civilised - after a fashion - although they later earned a reputation for being fierce warriors and for being extremely hairy.

Ancient Spain was rich in metals. As early as 1,900 BC, the Iberians were digging for them in the mines of Tartessos in the far south-west. Tartessos is mentioned in the Bible as *Tarshish*, a place of fabulous wealth. There were other Iberian settlements too, at Valencia, Tarragona and Sagunto, which went by the Iberian name of *Arse*.

Getting waisted

At one of their annual festivals, Iberian women measured each other's waists with a belt of a standard size. Any woman found to be too large was mocked by the others. It's not known what this standard size was.

If you're in Seville

The Carambola Treasure is a large collection of very beautiful gold jewellery from Tartessos. It's on display in the Archeological Museum of Seville, in María Luisa Park where an entire room is given over to it. The treasure was unearthed in 1958 while workmen were digging the foundations of a local sports centre.

It wasn't until 1,200 BC that the outside world discovered Tartessos. Around that date, traders from the eastern end of the Mediterranean came to trade for silver. They were brilliant sailors these eastern traders. They'd discovered that the position of the North Star is always almost due north and used it to find their way across the Mediterranean Sea, knowledge which they kept secret for centuries. Their ships were gaily painted, broad in the beam and rode high in the water

to give maximum space for cargo. The trade was so rich that on the return voyage their anchors were often cast of solid silver, or so the legends claimed. These traders came from Phoenicia in what is now Lebanon. Gradually the 'Phoenicians' put down roots in Iberia. They founded Cádiz around 1000 BC, and Malaga not long after. This makes Cádiz one of the oldest cities in Europe as well as one of the most fascinating.

Benidorm and the Ancient Greeks

In the late seventh century BC, a Greek trading ship was blown off course by a fierce gale while sailing south from Greece towards Ancient Egypt. The captain had to furl his sails and let his ship run west before the wind otherwise he'd have gone under. Lashed by wind and rain his small ship was driven right across the Mediterranean and out through the 'Pillars of Hercules', as the Strait of Gibraltar was then called. When the gale died down, he found himself out in the Atlantic Ocean - beyond the edge of the known world.

The Pillars of Hercules and the dollar

Gibraltar, on the southern tip of Spain, and the mountain of Hacho on the African shore opposite, were called the 'Pillars of Hercules' by the Ancient Greeks. They were the outer limit of the known world. Hercules, the mythical Greek hero, was said to have built the rocks. The two vertical lines on the US dollar sign derive from the Pillars of Hercules, as symbolised in the Spanish royal coat of arms on the seventeenth century Spanish peso.

The name of the captain was Kolaios. He's the first person we know by name in connection with Spain. In a sense, his voyage is when Spanish history really begins, i.e. the written history of known individuals. Kolaios managed to land his ship on the south-west coast of Spain. He then made his way inland to Tartessos where he traded his cargo, thus breaking the centuries-old monopoly of the Phoenicians. He made a vast profit on the goods he took back with him to Greece - sixty talents, around 1,500 kilograms of silver - a huge sum in those days, or nowadays come to that. He died a wealthy man.

News of Kolaios's epic voyage spread quickly among the Ancient Greeks, who realised that there were easy pickings to be had. Soon they were building trading cities along the west coast of Spain. Evidence of their settlements lies beneath the flip-flopped feet of tourists right along the Costa Blanca. Modern Benidorm is most likely the site of *Alonai*, an ancient Greek trading post, and Alonai is not far from the equally ancient Greek city of *Akra-Leuka* (White Summit) - Alicante to you and me.

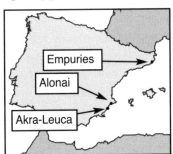

> ## Cartagena
>
> In 228 BC, descendants of the Phoenicians, then living in North Africa, founded the city of Cartagena in southern Spain (named after their home city of 'Carthage' near modern Tunis). The Carthaginians went into silver mining on their own account, rather than just trading for it with the native Iberians as their ancestors and as the Greeks had done. At its peak, their silver mine at Cartagena produced around 140 kilos of silver per day and employed up to 40,000 men.

Hispania

In the spring of 218 BC, a Carthaginian military genius called Hannibal, with an army of 40,000 which included Iberian soldiers and thirty-eight elephants, marched from Cartagena in southern Spain all the way to Italy, right

across what is now southern France, fighting most of the way. The story of how they crossed the snow-bound Alps (those that made it) is one of the epics of military history.

Hannibal's target was Rome. At that time Carthaginians

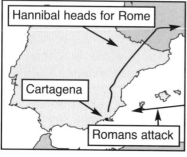

and Romans were at war for control of the western Mediterranean. It was because of Hannibal that the Romans first invaded Spain, in a massive counter-attack deep into Carthaginian-held territory late in 218 BC.

If you're in Valencia

There's a spectacular castle, at Xátiva near Valencia, where Hannibal's Iberian wife Imilce gave birth to a son shortly before he set off. An ancient statue, thought to be of Imilce herself, stands in the Plaza del Populo in Baeza, ninety kilometres north of Granada.

The Romans defeated the Carthaginians, just as they defeated almost everyone else. They then stayed on to defeat the Iberians, which took longer - over eighty years.

North of the Iberians lived the Celts, who'd invaded Spain from northern Europe around the seventh century BC. The Iberians were fierce but the Celts were fiercer. They believed in simple food, cold baths and fighting, in reverse order. Spanish Celts would later *volunteer* to be gladiators in the Roman arena. It took the Romans two hundred years to defeat the Celts as well as a mixed-race group called the Celt-Iberians.

Having defeated absolutely everybody, the Romans then settled down to rule Spain for six hundred years in total. Roman Spain became a rich and powerful province of the Roman Empire. Four Roman emperors were Spanish: Trajan, Hadrian, Antoninus Pius and Marcus Aurelius. Roman Spain also produced famous writers such as the poets Martial and Seneca, tutor to the Emperor Nero. Martial, who retired to a farm in Aragón, wrote in Latin but was very proud of his Spanish background. He described himself as a 'goat-bearded Iberian' - presumably he was one of the hairy ones.

If you're in Córdoba

Seneca was born in Córdoba. There's a statue of him in the Jewish quarter of the city.

What the Romans did for Spain

The Romans turned Spain into a highly civilised country. They established law and order, put on bloodthirsty circuses (not so civilised), and built bridges, roads, baths and aqueducts.

* *Roads*: over 360 towns were connected by over 12,000 miles of roads, the best road system Spain had until the twentieth century. The *Via Augusta* was a Roman road which started in Rome itself and finished in Cádiz.

* *Language*: based on Latin of course.

* *Aqueducts*: the aqueduct in Segovia is in such good condition that it could still carry water.

* *Judaism*: Jews came to Spain in large numbers around AD 117.

* *Bridges*:
  The bridge at Mérida has sixty arches and can still be walked over.

* *Christianity*:
  It began to take hold in the first century AD.

Santa Eulalia

Christianity first reached Spain during the Roman period. At first, it was frowned upon by the Roman authorities. Early Spanish Christians suffered for their beliefs, especially during the reign of the Emperor Nero (AD 54-68). Many of them died horribly, as in the case of a young girl called Eulalia who was torn to pieces with red hot pincers in Mérida.

Such torments are often lovingly documented in paintings in Spanish churches. Many Spaniards have a refreshingly hard-nosed attitude to gore.

If you're in Mérida

The most complete Roman ruins in Spain are at Mérida where Eulalia met her end, on the road from Madrid to Badajoz. Mérida, or 'Augusta Emerita' as it then was, was the capital of the Roman province of Lusitania, which included much of modern-day, central Portugal. Among other treasures, there's the stunning Roman bridge over the River Guadiana, an ampitheatre, a villa and a theatre. Eulalia's actual tomb is in the crypt of Barcelona Cathedral.

WHEN TOLEDO WAS TOP

A LAND FOR LOUTS

The naming of Andalusia

Or - Vandalusia

In the spring of AD 409, the peaceful communities of Roman Spain could still go about their business as if nothing was about to change. Craftsmen laid mosaic floors for new villas, slaves picked grapes for wine, others repaired the roads, local politicians gossiped in the forums. But times were troubled and people were anxious. The Roman Empire was under threat.

They were right to be anxious. Before the year was over, Roman Spain had folded. Hordes of large, fair-haired louts from northern Europe had rampaged south through Spanish towns and villages, an experience not entirely alien to the people of Malaga today. The louts in question were wild, Germanic tribesmen who'd crossed the frozen Rhine during winter and then fought their way down through what is now France. They invaded Spain at the invitation of an ambitious Roman general who wanted them to support his own push for power. Several tribes made the journey. Worst of them were the Vandals (where the modern word comes from). There weren't many Vandals but they wreaked mayhem.

The Romans were helpless against the marauding Vandals. They asked the Visigoths, another Germanic tribe, to come to their defence. The Visigoths sported long hair and massive, primitive jewellery and loved fighting, but they were at least Christians, unlike many other Germanic tribesmen who still worshipped pagan gods and went in for human sacrifice. In fact the Visigoths were partly Romanised, having fought for the Roman Empire on previous occasions.

The Visigoths drove the Vandals into southern Spain (Andalusia = Vandalusia) and then right out of Europe into North Africa. They also mopped up the other barbarians, leaving only the native Spanish. And *then*, seeing as there was no Roman army left worth speaking of - they decided to stay.

Catholicism comes of age

The Visigoths established their own barbarian kingdom in place of the Roman province of *Hispania*. The Visigoth capital was Toledo where they built a church.

If you're near Venta de Baños

There are very few Visigoth churches left in Spain. The best is the Basilica of San Juan Bautista, built in 661, in Baños de Cerrato, a village outside Venta de Baños, thirty-five kilometres north of Valladolid on the road to Burgos. It's reckoned to be the oldest church in Spain.

Also, the Visigothic mass is still celebrated at 9.30 every day in the Capilla Mozarábe in Toledo Cathedral: the only place in the world where it's still celebrated.

The Visigoths never integrated with their newly-conquered subjects although they tried desperately later on and even learned Latin. The Visigoths and the Romanised Spaniards were different types of Christian. Most Spaniards were *Roman Catholics* but the Visigoths were *Arians*. Among other things, Arians didn't believe that Christ was as important as God. This meant that Spanish Catholics loathed the Visigoths as a matter of religious principle. There's a wonderfully vicious description by a Spanish Catholic of the Visigoth King Leovigild (reigned AD 569-586):

> *His forehead was savage, his eyes were wild, his expression was hateful, his movements were violent. He was depraved in his mind, of sinister character, of lying tongue and obscene speech ... he was utterly devoid of inner virtues, he was malformed both within and without, he had no goodness in him whatsoever, he was overflowing with evil, criminal, and totally reckless of eternal death.*

The loathing rubbed both ways. Visigoth kings persecuted their Catholic subjects whenever they got the chance, which was frequently, King Leovigild himself being particularly unpleasant. But then in 589, Leovigild's second son, Reccared, came to the throne. Reccared converted and became a Catholic. That year, Roman Catholicism became the official religion of Spain - as it has been ever since.

How Gibraltar got its name

Old songs and chronicles relate that, towards the end of the Visigoth period, a certain Count Julian was governor of Ceuta, a Visigoth outpost on the African coast opposite Gibraltar. Julian was a bitter enemy of King Roderic, a new king who'd only recently been chosen to rule by the Visigoth nobles. Roderic had seduced Julian's daughter - or so the songs and chronicles say.

Out of spite and to revenge himself on his enemy, in AD 710 Julian invited an Arab army into Spain in support of a rival claim for the throne.

This was a disaster for the Visigoths. The Arabs were extremely dangerous. Mohammed the Prophet had died only eighty years before and they were fired up with Islamic zeal. Converting the world to Islam tied in well with less holy ambitions such as the desire for loot.

Late in 711, an Arab-led army landed in Gibraltar commanded by a war leader called Tariq. 'Gibraltar' comes from *'Jebel Tariq'* which means 'Rock of Tariq' in Arabic. Roderic rushed south to defend his kingdom. Sometime in 712, the Arab and Visigoth armies met beside the banks of the River Guadalete between Algeciras and Jerez.

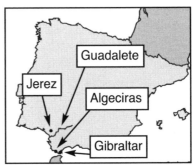

The Visigoths had gone soft. They were no longer the fierce, barbarian warriors of former years. King Roderic directed his forces while lying on a cart of ivory drawn by two white mules. When all was lost, he ran away and was drowned in the blood-stained waters of the Guadalete, weighed down by his golden crown and his silk robes.

It was the end of the Visigoths - and the start of nearly eight hundred years of Islam in Spain.

ANDALUSIA
RATHER MOORISH

A dash of Islam

Islamic warriors poured into Spain following the defeat of Roderic. They were led by Arabs but most of them were recently converted Berbers (from *barbarus*, the Latin for 'barbarian') native inhabitants of North Africa, the last major ingredient in the Spanish national soup. Up to 200,000 of this motley crew followed Tariq into Spain and soon the whole peninsula was in their grasp, apart from a few pockets of resistance in the northern hills.

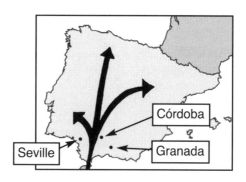

From Córdoba to Granada via Seville
The three stages

Muslim Spain (or 'Moorish' Spain from an old word for North African) happened in three stages, each based round one of the three southern cities of Córdoba, Seville and Granada. Each city took centre stage in turn and each produced a new flowering of Islamic culture.

1. Córdoba 756-1010
2. Seville: 1010-1248
3. Granada: 1248-1492.

Córdoba

Córdoba, with its beautiful Roman bridge, was the largest city in western Europe during its time as the Muslim capital. It was an oasis in a medieval desert. In the tenth century, as many as 200,000 people lived there. This was at a time when the population of London was around 10,000. At a time when the citizens of most European cities had to find their way home at night with a lantern and armed with a cudgel in case of robbers, Córdoba, the 'Pearl of the Universe' as described by a German nun called Hrotswitha, had street lights and paved roads. Water was piped to the public fountains. There were gardens, palaces, beautiful mosques, schools, a university (the first in Europe) and 400,000 manuscripts in the great library. Arab, Christian and Jewish scholars flocked there, lured by the civilised lifestyle. Ancient Greek manuscripts were studied and knowledge of ancient Greece and the Arab world became available in Europe for the first time since the fall of the Roman Empire.

The arm of the rulers of Córdoba stretched far beyond the city itself. They controlled all of Andalusia and most of Spain. The Moors were superb farmers. They introduced rice, sugar cane, hard wheat, cotton, oranges, lemons, limes, aubergines, bananas, pomegranates, watermelons, artichokes and spinach. Many Spanish words borrowed from Arabic are to do with agriculture.

If you're in Córdoba

The ruins of the huge palace/city of the last Caliph of Córdoba lie seven kilometres outside the city proper. It was built by Caliph Abd ar-Rahman III, starting in 936, and is named 'Medina Azahara' after his favourite wife, az-Zahra. The work took twenty-five years to complete. The complex is over 2,000 metres long and more than 9,000 metres wide. At its peak it housed over 12,000 people and a small zoo. It had three hundred baths and innumerable marble fountains.

In 1010, it was comprehensively sacked by North African mercenary troops and by the townsfolk of Córdoba, following the death of the legenday Al-Mansur, and never recovered.

What Europe got from the Spanish Muslims

In the long term, Europe did very well out of the Arab conquest of Spain. Through Córdoba and then Seville and Granada, it got:

* *'Algebra'*   * *'Arabic' numerals*

* *Zero (an Indian invention originally)*   * *The decimal system*

* *Paper (originally invented in China)*   * *Universities*

* *New types of fruit and veg.*

* *Olé! Olé! (means Allah! Allah!)*

Caliphs and emirs

Moorish Spain was part of the Islamic world empire. Its military commanders (Emirs) answered to Baghdad, where Mohammed's successors, the Caliphs, ruled in splendour. In theory, there could only ever be one Caliph ruling all the lands of Islam and he gave the orders. In practice, Baghdad had virtually no say over what went on in Spain which was too far away.

The first dynasty of Caliphs had been the Ummayad family who ruled the Islamic world from Damascus in Syria. They were overthrown in 750 by

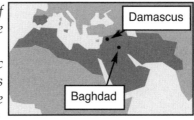

the Abbasid family who used the captured Ummayad wealth to build the new Islamic capital city of Baghdad, in what is now Iraq. The Abbasids slaughtered all the Ummayads they could lay their hands on. Only one senior male Ummayad escaped. Aged nineteen, this survivor fled to Córdoba where he managed to seize power. His name was Abd ar-Rahman.

Abd ar-Rahman became the first Emir of Córdoba in 756. Unsurprisingly, ar-Rahman's descendents were less than friendly towards the Abbasid caliphs who had pushed their ancestors from supreme power. Nearly two hundred years later, in 929, Abd ar-Rahman III, a descendant of Abd ar-Rahman I, declared himself to be Caliph of Córdoba in his own right and no longer just an emir. He thus broke the rule that there could only ever be one Caliph in the Islamic world. From then on the Ummayad Caliphate of Córdoba was independent of the rest of the Muslim world.

Mozárabes

Church bells and plonk

Mozárabes were Christians who lived in Spain under Muslim rule. Muslims complained about Mozárabe church bells, their pigs and their wine shops, but the Mozárabes were useful. Muslims would visit Mozárabe monasteries if they wanted alcohol, which many of them did and, more importantly, the Mozárabes paid extra tax.

Muslim tolerance was amazing - for the period. The Moors were confident that Islam was the only true religion and that it would conquer the world eventually. They saw the Mozárabes as foolish followers of a similar religion, to be scorned rather than persecuted. When the Moors first captured Córdoba, they *bought* half of its fine Visigothic church, St. Vincent's, from the Christians. Far from razing it to the ground, for nearly fifty years they allowed it to be shared by Christians and Muslims alike. It wasn't until 785 that Abd ar-Rahman I bought the other half and built the magnificent Mosque of Córdoba.

Likewise the Moors tolerated Jews. The Jewish population of Spain increased once the Visigoths were out of the way.

If you're near León

The largest Mozárabe building in Spain is the beautiful church of San Miguel de Escalada, about twenty kilometres east of León in the north of Spain. It was completed in 913 by refugee monks from Muslim Córdoba, using traditional techniques copied from the great mosque at Córdoba including the horseshoe arch, a typical Mozárabe feature.

> **Blondes**
>
> *Blonde* gallegas, *Christian women from Galicia, were popular with Moorish rulers. They were frequently demanded as tribute. Moorish harems were full of them - to the extent that the later Caliphs often had blue eyes due to having blonde mothers and grandmothers.*

The Scourge of the Christians

As the years of Muslim rule went by, Christian and Muslim attitudes hardened. In 976, a twelve-year-old boy became Caliph in Córdoba, and the reins of power were grasped by a powerful military commander known as Al-Mansur ('the Victorious'). He made sure that the young Caliph lived a life of enfeebling luxury so as to keep him from power. In fifty-seven brutal expeditions, Al-Mansur sacked all the major Christian cities of northern Spain and in 997 he sacked the great shrine of Santiago de Compostela, the emotional heart of Christian Spain. The bells of Santiago were carted back to Córdoba where they were melted down and made into candelabra for the Great Mosque.

Christian vengeance had to wait until 1236, when Córdoba was captured by King Ferdinand III of Castile, the Saint. He forced his Muslim prisoners to cart what was left of the bells and other treasures back to Santiago.

Tangerines

In 1085, Morocco, just over the water in North Africa, was in the grip of a warlike, Islamic, religious movement which controlled a vast African empire stretching from Senegal in the south to the Mediterranean Sea in the north. The fanatical warriors of this movement called themselves *Almoravids*, meaning 'those vowed to God'. When the Almoravids went into battle they were unbeatable. Enemies often fled at the sound of their huge war drums without ever coming to blows.

The Almoravids were very different to the civilised Muslims of Spain. The Almoravid leader Yusuf stank of camels, dressed in skins and spoke bad Arabic. Spanish Muslims looked down on the Almoravids and called them 'Tangerines' (still grown in Algeria) - although only behind their backs.

Although Spanish Muslims looked down on the Almoravids, in 1085 they found that they needed them. Al-Mansur had died in 1002, 'buried in hell' as a Christian writer put it, and the Córdoban Caliphate had split up into tiny statelets, twenty-six to begin with. These 'Taifa' states (petty kingdoms) were hopelessly weak and at the mercy of Christian kingdoms to the north. In 1085 Toledo was captured by the Christian King Alfonso VI of Castile. It looked as if all of Andalusia was about to fall. Shocked to the core, the Taifa kings, led by the Emir of Seville, asked the Almoravids for help.

Yusuf, the Almoravid leader, landed in Spain in 1085 at

the head of a formidable army. He smashed Alfonso's Castilians at the Battle of al-Zallaquah near Badajoz in 1086 - then, having failed to recapture Toledo, he gobbled up Andalusia (Muslim Spain) instead.

Seville

Andalusia soon worked its magic on the fearsome Almoravids. They changed from fierce fanatics to soft sybarites in the space of a generation. A hundred years later, they were pushed aside by a new wave of fanatics from North Africa. This lot were even more fanatical. They called themselves *Almohads*, meaning 'those who believe in the unity of God'. The Almohads defeated the Almoravids and conquered most of Andalusia including Seville. Then Andalusia worked its magic yet again and the Almohads too went soft.

Seville now took over as top city of Andalusia. The Almohads built palaces and towers in Seville. They repaired the old Roman aqueduct. They built quays along the banks of the Guadalquivir and large warehouses. In 1170, work began on a massive mosque and in 1171 they began work on their palatial fortress, the Alcázar.

If you're in Seville
The Giralda Tower, built of decorative bricks, was once the minaret of the great mosque of Seville. It's one of the loveliest Muslim buildings in Spain, although largely rebuilt. After the Christians took the city it became the bell tower of the cathedral. It's open to the public.

Apart from their tremendous building programme, the Almohads encouraged learning throughout Andalusia. Philosophers such as Ibn Rushd - Averroës as he's commonly known - and the Jewish Moses Maimonides (1125-1204) flourished at this time. Both these men had a major impact on later Christian philosophers.

If you're in Córdoba

Moses Maimonides was born in Córdoba. There's a statue of him in the Jewish quarter, not far from the statue of Seneca.

The beginning of the end

While the Almohads and their successors were building mosques and encouraging learning, the Christian warriors in the north sharpened their swords and got on with what Christian warriors did best - fighting. On Monday 16 July 1212, Christian knights of Spain under Alfonso VIII of Castile, backed up by crusaders from elsewhere in Europe, marched south from Toledo. They smashed the Muslims at Las Navas de Tolosa far to the south, attacking from behind after they'd been shown the way by a Mozárabe shepherd. The Christians followed up their success in the years which followed. Alfonso VIII's successor, Ferdinand III of Castile, took first Córdoba (1236) and then Seville (1248).

Now most of Spain was Christian, for the first time since the age of the Visigoths. The great mosque of Seville was demolished, apart from the famous Giralda Tower, and a cathedral was built in its place. Ferdinand III is still there in Seville Cathedral. Three times a year, his bejewelled casket is ceremoniously exposed to public view together with his kingly robes and sceptre.

> ## The siege of Seville
> *The siege of Seville took sixteen agonising months. The Moorish defenders used state-of-the-art catapults to hurl massive stones from the ramparts at the soldiers of Ferdinand III. The Moorish bowmen could kill horses in full armour. In reply, Ferdinand destroyed the surrounding countryside. For days on end the streets of the besieged city were dark as night because of the soot and smoke. Starvation eventually brought the Moors to their knees. When the time came to surrender, the defenders were little more than skin and bone.*

Granada

> *The Sabika hill sits like a garland on Granada's brow,*
> *In which the stars would be entwined,*
> *And the Alhambra (God preserve it)*
> *Is the ruby set above that garland.**

After the fall of Seville, a stream of desperate refugees fled east to Granada, the only Muslim kingdom of any size left in Andalusia. As many as a hundred thousand trod the weary road, taking with them what possessions they could carry.

Granada was now a tiny island in a hostile, Christian ocean. Amazingly, it held out for another 244 years - until 1492 when it was finally captured by Ferdinand and Isabella.

*From a poem by Ibn Zamrak, chief minister of Mohammed V of Granada (1354-59 & 1362-91).

Granada is still one of the loveliest cities in Spain, surrounded by mountains and in the middle of a lush plain, still irrigated by water brought from the mountains on the old Moorish aqueducts. As with Córdoba and Seville, medieval Granada was far in advance of Christian cities of the time such as Paris and London. With the help of the new arrivals from Seville, it soon became one of the richest cities in Europe. The houses were spacious, there were paved roads and water was piped around the city. There were even toilets flushed by running water.

The jewel within this jewel was the Alhambra, the 'Red Palace', started back in AD 890, on the Sabika hill above the city, and extended over the centuries by Granada's rulers. It's one of the finest buildings in the world.

The end of Muslim Spain
Granada was able to hold out against the Christians because it was a fortress kingdom. Thousands of watchtowers kept guard day and night, a chain of castles protected its borders. It had excellent soldiers and cunning rulers.

The watchtowers, the castles, the brave soldiers, the cunning rulers, strong allies from Morocco - none of them could save Granada for ever. It was too small and by 1492, Christian Spain was too powerful. The Christians had come a long way since their defeated Visigoth remnants fled before the Arab army of Tariq back in 711. By 1492 the 'Catholic Monarchs' Ferdinand and Isabella led a powerful army and a united country.

When Granada surrendered, Ferdinand and Isabella dressed up in Moorish robes to receive the keys to the city. Perhaps this was meant to reassure the inhabitants that they could continue their Muslim ways. If so, it was a joke in poor taste. Within ten years all Spanish Muslims were forced either to convert to Christianity or to leave the country. Muslim Spain was all but eradictated.

MEN WITH LONG BEARDS
COMPOSTELA OR BUST

The *Reconquista*

So who *were* the Christians who took Granada? How did they fight back from abject defeat in 711 to total victory in 1492?

Obviously, it didn't happen overnight. The Arabs took just seven years to conquer Spain (711-718), but the Christians took over *seven hundred* years to win it back (718-1492), a process called the *Reconquista*.

Asturias

A savage ass fights back

In AD 718, seven years after the Arab invasion, an Islamic army marched into the Christian-held Cantabrian mountains in north-west Spain, intent on crushing this last pocket of Christian resistance. In the valley of Covadonga deep in the hills, the Arab army was defeated by a bunch of hillmen led by a Cantabrian chieftain called Pelayo, that 'savage ass' as one Arab writer described him. Christian chroniclers describe the odds as being 31 to 40,000 against the Christians. An absurd exaggeration, but still, Covadonga was where the Christian fightback began. Pelayo didn't stop the Arab advance into Europe. The

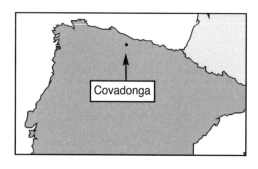

Covadonga

If you're in Asturias
Covadonga, 11 kilometres south of Cangas in central Asturias, has become a place of pilgrimage and a major shrine. Mass is celebrated daily in a cave high above the valley. In this cave, Pelayo is said to have sheltered and prayed before descending to give battle in the valley below. There's a large, pink, nineteenth-century basilica nearby and a small museum.

Arabs were finally checked at Poitiers in 732 by the Frenchman Charles Martel (The Hammer). But Pelayo went on to found the small, independent kingdom of Asturias in the only part of Spain which never submitted to Muslim rule. From this tiny nut grew the kingdoms of Galicia and León and finally Castile and modern Spain itself. In honour of Pelayo's stubborn resistance, the heir to the Spanish throne is always called 'Prince of Asturias', rather as the heir to the British Throne is called Prince of Wales. The kings of Spain have always dreamed of a direct link, via Pelayo, to the old Visigoth kingdom, although, in actual fact, Pelayo was more likely a local leader than a member of the Visigoth aristocracy.

Consolidation
In the eight century, when the Muslims were strong and the Christians were weak, several tiny Christian kingdoms were crammed into northern Spain. The story of how these expanded and joined together to form bigger kingdoms and how the bigger kingdoms then joined together to form even bigger kingdoms is the story of the *Reconquista*. At the end of this process of consolidation, Castile emerged as the biggest and most powerful Christian kingdom. Finally, under Ferdinand and Isabella, Castile joined with Aragón and Spain became one big, powerful Christian country.

Eight steps to power

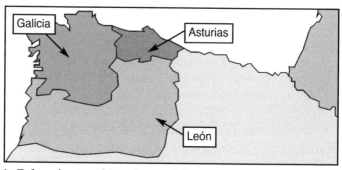

1. Pelayo's tiny kingdom of Asturias became a refuge for Christians fleeing their Muslim conquerors in the south. Its population grew. The kingdom expanded west into the region of Galicia and south into the plain of León. In the 800s, it split up into the separate kingdoms of León, Galicia and the original Asturias.

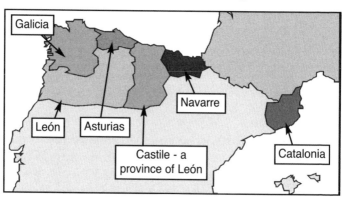

2. Leon then expanded south - and also east, into Castile. Elsewhere, the Basque kingdom of Navarre took shape and the Emperor Charlemagne took over what was to become Catalonia (801). By AD 900, the map of Christian Spain looked like this. (Asturias is shown separately but had been absorbed by León.)

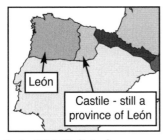

3. In 914 Galicia became part of the Kingdom of León, now the most powerful kingdom.

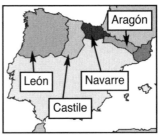

4. in 1035 Castile became an independent kingdom and Aragón split off from Navarre.

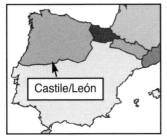

5. In 1072 Castile and León were reunited.

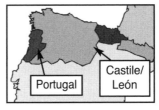

6. In 1139 Portugal split off from the León part of Castile/León, and became an independent state.

7. In 1162 Aragón and Catalonia were united, forming a powerful state.

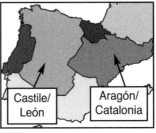

8. By 1230 there were two growing centres of power: Castile/León and Aragón/Catalonia.

The coming of Castile

The seven-hundred year *Reconquista* wasn't one, incredibly long war. There were many periods of peace between the periods of violence. Quite often, Christian kings fought *with* Muslim rulers against other Christian kings. Sometimes the Muslims gained the upper hand. But mostly, it was Christians who attacked and Muslims who retreated.

Each time the Muslims retreated, they destroyed the land they left behind them. This created a huge swathe of desolate no man's land between Christian north and Muslim south. The swathe of desolate land moved gradually south as the Christian states expanded, so that the Christian settlers always planted their new villages and farms in deserted territory - dangerous, frontier land. The settlers needed to be on constant lookout against Muslim counter-attack. And when attacks came, they needed strong defences to retreat into, and to attack from in their turn.

This is why the empty, barren landscape of central Spain is dotted with castles and why it's called Castile - which means 'land of castles'.

If you're near Valencia

Mudéjars were Muslims who stayed behind to work for the Christians. Mudéjar churches are often very beautiful. They made use of decorative brickwork and tiles. One of the best places to see Mudéjar architecture is in the small Aragonese town of Teruel about 150 kilometres north-west of Valencia. It has two fine, free-standing Mudéjar church towers along with other treasures.

Santiago de Compostela

One night in AD 813, a solitary hermit in remote Galicia saw a star shining over a massive oak tree which grew on a lonely hill. For several nights he watched the star and claimed he could hear heavenly music ringing in his ears. He reported his experience to the  local bishop and the bishop decided to investigate. Beneath the tree they found an altar and human bones. Three bodies had been buried together and one of them had had its head chopped off.

King Alfonso II of Asturias was informed about this discovery and he too visited the site. He consulted with the priests and other wise men of his little kingdom, and it was decided that the bones of the decapitated body must be those of St James, Apostle of Jesus, beheaded by King Herod in Jerusalem in AD 43, when the Roman Empire was at its height. Ancient tradition said that the followers of St James had preserved his body, loaded it on a ship and taken it from Palestine to Spain for burial.

> **If you're in Santiago**
> You can still see the silver urn which contains the bones of St James in the great cathedral of *Santiago de Compostela* - 'Saint James of the Field of the Star' - built on the very spot where the hermit found them.

Santiago de Compostela became the most important place of pilgrimage in Europe. The cult of St James acted as fuel for the Christian crusade against Islam and for the *Reconquista*. By the eleventh century, St James was known

43

as *Santiago Matamores* - 'Saint James the Moor-Killer' because of the help he was thought to give in battle. His name became the battle-cry of Spanish knights. The real St James, Apostle of the Religion of Peace, must have turned in his grave - or he would have if he'd still had a grave to turn in.

Bone people

St. James's bones were dug up in 1700, when an English invasion was feared during the lead-up to the War of the Spanish Succession (1701-15). They were reburied in a secret location along with two other bodies. The three sets of bones were rediscovered in 1879 during restoration work. Those of St James were identified by means of a piece of Santiago's skull from a church in Tuscany which exactly fitted a hole in the main skull. He's now kept in the crypt beneath the main altar at Compostela.

The Pilgrim Way

The cult of St. James was a Europe-wide phenomenon. Throughout the Middle Ages, vast numbers of pilgrims from all over Europe poured into Santiago de Compostela. As they trudged across northern Spain they camped and slept at inns along the way. Their accounts give us some vivid descriptions of the Spanish people, not all of them complimentary. The Pilgrims' Way passed through Navarre where the Basques drew special criticism from a French pilgrim:

Truly, these people are disgustingly dressed, and they eat and drink disgustingly. The way they eat makes you think of pigs or dogs ... This is a savage race, puffed up with evil, dark in colour, vile of face, depraved, twisted, faithless and corrupt, over-sexed, drunken, given to violence, savage and wild, lying and criminal, irreligious and hard, cruel and argumentative, strangers to anything good ...

None of which is a comment on the modern Basques of course, and it was no doubt unfair at the time. You can still walk the Pilgrim Way, and most Basques are delightful people.

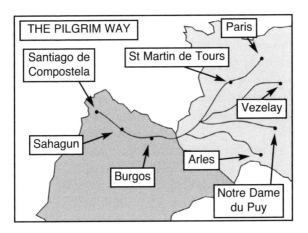

Fighting fathers

The petty kingdoms of Christian Spain were often at each other's throats, but one thing united them - the long crusade to recover 'their' land from the Moors. This was the glue which held Christian Spain together for seven hundred years. Brotherhoods of armed monks were formed. Men joining these brotherhoods swore to dedicate their lives to the struggle. An oath taken by members of a brotherhood founded in 1122 began:

We vow never to live at peace with the pagans (Muslims) but to devote all our days to fighting them ...

45

Three of these brotherhoods, the orders of Calatrava, Alcántara and Santiago, became very powerful and rich in later years.

If you're in Extremadura

The headquarters of the brotherhood of Alcántara was in the huge Convent of San Benito in the town of Alcántara in Extremadura, near the border with Portugal. The existing building is mainly sixteenth century and was never finished but what there is of it is massive - the fighting brothers were wealthy. It's open to the public most weekdays.

In all Medieval countries, religion ruled peoples lives, above all in Spain due to the demands of the *Reconquista*. Along with the brotherhoods of armed monks, the Spanish church became extremely powerful, especially after 1083 when the Pope declared Spain to be an area of 'Holy War'. This gave a green light to the more aggressive clergy - of whom there were many. Some bishops owned castles, some even had their own private armies and several led their troops into battle personally, although, as in the rest of Europe, they had to kill with a mace or club because stabbing with a sword was thought unseemly. It was easy to finance such priestly escapades because the clergy paid no taxes.

El Cid
'He of the great beard'

The Cantar de mio Cid *(Song of my Lord) was written around 1140 which makes it the oldest epic poem in the Spanish language. It tells the story of the Castilian knight, Rodrigo Diaz de Vivar -* El Cid *(c.1043-1099). 'Cid' comes from the Arabic* sidi *meaning 'lord'.*

The poem gives a vivid picture of early medieval Spain. In the poem, Cid, 'he of the great beard', is tall, honourable and brave and often wears his long beard in a net so as not to be dishonoured by having it tweaked. There's plenty of gore and plenty of realism. After one battle he returns to his wife and daughters with his sword dripping blood. The poem describes in graphic detail how the blood runs right up to the hilt and along his arm to the elbow.

Due to an edgy relationship with his king Alfonso VI of Castile, El Cid spent much of his life in exile, fighting sometimes for Muslim kings and sometimes against them. The high point of his career came when he took Valencia from the Muslims (1093-4) and defeated the fearsome Almoravids. Alfonso should have been the more famous of the pair, being the conqueror of Toledo and a powerful king as well, but the Cantar de mio Cid *is such a beautiful poem that it's El Cid who was immortalised.*

If you're in Madrid
You can see El Cid's sword in the *Museo del Ejército* or Army Museum in Madrid, just to the side of the big *Museo del Prado*. It's a superb Arab weapon and very well made, probably a gift from a grateful Arab ally, if not captured in battle.

To wash or not to wash

Many things set medieval Christians and Muslims apart: mosques and churches, drinking or not drinking alcohol, women kept in the harem or not kept in the harem. One of the most obvious differences was dirt. Muslims were clean; Christians didn't believe in washing, at least not often. To Christians, dirt was a sign of holiness. Men spoke of the 'odour of sanctity' in reference to the smell of unwashed bodies. When the Visigoths first took over, they destroyed Roman baths, believing that they made people soft. Muslims used to say of Christians that they were sprinkled with holy water at baptism and so were relieved of ever having to wash again.

Saints
Some images of saints show them sitting in their own excrement as a sign of their holiness.

The differences between the two sides made it difficult for them to accept each other but not impossible. Quite a few Christians spoke and read Arabic and wore comfortable Moorish clothes in the privacy of their own homes.

Alas, as time went by, attitudes hardened on both sides of the religious divide, especially after the Almoravid and Almohad invasions from Africa. Whereas Spanish

Muslims were broadly the same racial mix as Christians, the Almoravids and Almohads were more African. They looked different. Also, being fanatics, they were nastier to the Christians in their territory. In response, the Christians increased their persecution of Muslims and Jews in Christian territory. A vicious circle developed.

Alfonso X the Wise

Alfonso X the Wise *(el Sabio)* of Castile (1252-84) was a wise and noble king. He loved to study science and literature. He wore silk robes embroidered with gold and precious stones, and his court at Toledo was superior to courts in France, England and Germany.

When he came to the throne, Córdoba and Seville had only recently fallen to Castile (1236 and 1248 respectively) so he was inheriting a kingdom which had become half Moorish almost overnight. And the Moorish half was the best half. The Muslims were better engineers, scholars, doctors, armourers, manufacturers and farmers than the Christians. Christian Castile was like a snake that had swallowed its larger prey whole and now must digest it.

Alfonso was no Christian fanatic. He wanted Christian Castile to soak up all that was best from its new Muslim subjects - even if he had to rely on Jews and Arabs to do it for him. He made Toledo into a centre of learning. Large numbers of Arabic and ancient Greek texts were translated into Latin, mainly by Jewish and Muslim scholars. Once in Latin, they became available to the wider world of European scholars, Latin then being the international language. This fuelled the rebirth of European learning known as the Renaissance.

Counting sheep

Spanish Muslims were excellent all-round farmers and gardeners, but the Christians tended to specialise in sheep. Sheep were well suited to the high, dry plains of Castile and to the bleak conditions of no man's land as the *Reconquista* moved south.

Sheep tended to get lost. They wandered off into the wide, empty hills. In the early Middle Ages, Christian shepherds organised themselves into *mestas*, small groups of men who met to sort out problems such as who owned which stray sheep. In 1273, Alfonso combined these local *mestas* into an efficient national association. Taxes on sheep were an important source of his income. The national *Mesta* was good for sheep rearing and therefore good for the royal treasury.

Alfonso the Wise's scholarly efforts were an excellent thing - not so the *Mesta*. It became a hugely powerful organisation. Every year vast flocks of sheep were herded across Spain from northern to southern pastures and back again, eating everthing in their path like swarms of locusts. The interests of sheep were put before the interests of other more productive farmers who had to let the sheep wander across their land, whether they wanted to or not.

THE SPANISH EMPIRE
MADRID AND THE SPIDER'S WEB

I saw no animals on the island, only parrots*.

Vows in Valladolid

It was 1469. Alfonso V, the middle-aged king of Portugal, needed a bride. He had his eye on Isabella, young heir to the throne of Castile. Castile and Portugal would form a powerful bloc if they were united by royal marriage. Also, Isabella had auburn hair and sparkling, green-blue eyes. He fancied her.

Isabella wasn't interested. She'd set her heart on Ferdinand, heir to the crown of Aragón. Ferdinand was young, good-looking and extremely cunning and clever. Because many of Castile's powerful noblemen backed the Alfonso marriage, Isabella's envoys travelled in secrecy to the Aragonese court at Zaragoza where they invited Ferdinand to meet her at Valladolid.

To avoid trouble, Ferdinand made his way to Valladolid disguised as a servant, waiting on the rest of his party in the hotels and inns when they stopped at night. Once the young couple finally met, the attraction was instant. They were married soon after, in a small palace right there in

*From Columbus's account of his landing on Hispaniola to their Catholic majesties Ferdinand and Isabella.

town. Because they were not-so-distant cousins, they needed the Pope's permission to marry - Ferdinand's father and a friendly bishop forged a document which appeared to give the Pope's approval.

That was the beginning of modern Spain. And that's why Spain is now a mixture of Castile and Aragón, not of Castile and Portugal, which could easily have happened.

If you're in Valladolid
The marriage of Ferdinand and Isabella took place in the 'Rich Room' of the Palacio de los Viveros in central Valladolid.

Catholic kings

Ferdinand and Isabella had a very successful marriage. They ruled together as the 'Catholic Kings', a title given to them by the Pope. Together they brought wealth and unity to Spain.

Together, Castile and Aragón were far more powerful than Granada, the last remaining Muslim kingdom. Ferdinand and Isabella soon found reason to pick an argument. They invaded Granada with a large army and the Muslim forces retreated into Granada city itself. It was at this point that Ferdinand and Isabella built their military camp of Santa Fé just outside the city, in order to pursue the siege in comfort.

The Catholic Monarchs were both pious Catholics, but Isabella was specially pious. When Columbus met her on that fateful winter's day in Santa Fé in 1491, he spoke persuasively of the heathen masses he would discover and how they would be converted to Christianity. Also, wealth arising from the voyage could be used to finance a crusade for the recapture of Jerusalem from the Muslims.

(Columbus thought big.) All this was strong wine for Isabella's pious soul.

When Columbus finally set sail in 1492, Granada had fallen. Catholic Spain was now riding the crest of a wave. Anything seemed possible. Three months later, an edict was issued expelling all Jews from the country.

When he returned, Columbus travelled to Barcelona where Ferdinand and Isabella were then holding court. He was weighed down with gifts of gold and pearls. He showed them exotic, brightly-coloured parrots and six 'Indians' from the Caribbean in all their finery to prove what he'd found. He told Ferdinand and Isabella that he'd found a new route to China, as promised. But he hadn't of course, he'd discovered America. His gift to Spain was far greater than he imagined and far greater than a mere trade route. What he'd actually given was the opportunity for a vast, new empire in the west.

Christian Spain, hardened by seven hundred years of the *Reconquista*, was ready to seize the opportunity.

If you're in Seville
The posthumous voyages of Christopher Columbus
Columbus died in Valladolid in 1506. Shortly after, his body was dug up and taken to Seville. In the 1544, he was dug up again and shipped to the island of Hispaniola, 'the land that I loved the most'. In 1795 when the French were about to capture the island, he was dug up for the third time and taken to Cuba. And in 1899, just before Cuba became independent, he was dug up for the fourth time and shipped back to Seville, where he's now buried in the cathedral. His massive monument is the first thing you see on entering*.

---

*At the time of going to print - new research indicates that the body in the tomb at Seville may not be Columbus's but, possibly, that of his son.

53

The Spanish Empire

At its height the Spanish Empire included all of Portugal's colonies as well as Spanish colonies and Hapsburg territories in Europe.

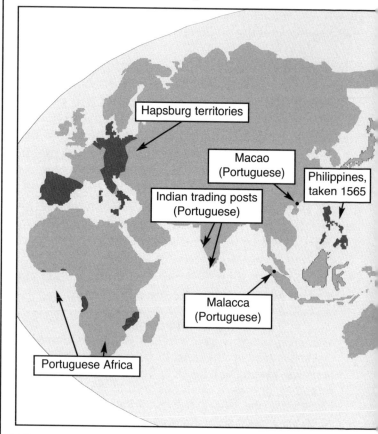

Conquistadors

On 8 November 1519, a tiny army of 508 Spanish soldiers with 16 horses and about 1,000 native 'Indian' allies to back them up mounted a pass between two volcanoes high in central Mexico. They paused to recover their

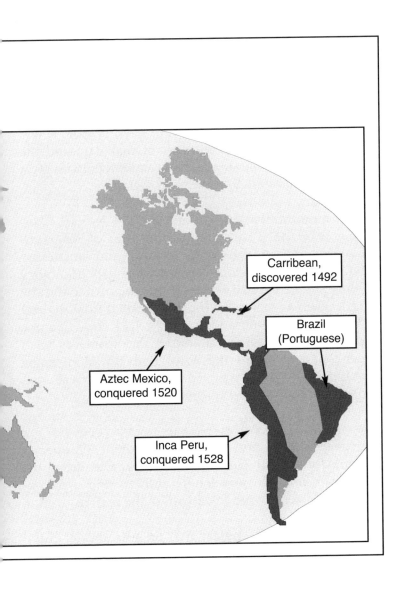

Carribean,
discovered 1492

Brazil
(Portuguese)

Aztec Mexico,
conquered 1520

Inca Peru,
conquered 1528

breath, and then gazed in wonder. Below them lay a wide plateau. In the centre of the plateau was a lake. In the centre of the lake, across a series of islands, both man-made and artificial, spread an immense city. Other satellite cities were strung around its banks like planets round the sun.

The lake was Texcoco and the city was Tenochtitlán, capital of the Aztec Empire. Tenochtitlán was no savage encampment. With a population of over 100,000, it was larger than most European cities of that date and the centre of a great civilisation. It had beautiful palaces, great temples, cool gardens and excellent sanitation.

Within months, Tenochtitlán and the whole, vast Aztec Empire were in the hands of that tiny army of Spaniards, following one of the most reckless and audacious conquests in world history. The Spaniards had technology on their side. They had horses, iron, gunpowder and the wheel, whereas the native Indians, isolated from the rest of humanity for thousands of years, had none of these things. But even more important, the Spaniards were super-confident - and the Aztec Emperor Montezuma thought that they were gods whose arrival was prophecied by the Aztec religion.

The Spanish leader was Hernan Cortez (1485-1547), a native of Medellin, near the old Roman town of Merida in Extremadura. He'd launched his expedition from the island of Cuba. He was tough, ruthless and a devout Catholic, in fact, a typical Spaniard of the period.

Twelve years later, in January 1531, an even smaller group of Spaniards landed from a single ship on the coast of what is now Peru. There were just 180 of them with 37 horses. This miniscule but utterly ruthless army marched inland, into the heartland of the Inca Empire which then covered a vast section of eastern South America. When he heard of their arrival, the Inca Emperor Atahualpa was curious and invited them to come and meet him. They presented Atahualpa with a Bible and called on him to become a Christian and to submit to King Charles I of Spain. Atahualpa dropped the Bible, whereupon the Spanish fired their canon into his six thousand unarmed attendants. They cut down the imperial bodyguard with their steel swords and dragged Atahualpa from his golden litter.

The ransom the Spanish demanded for the release of Atahualpa was a pile of gold large enough to fill a nearby room. Five months later and when the ransom was almost paid, they gave him a choice: either be burned alive or else convert to Christianity, in which case, he would only be strangled. Understandably, Atahualpa chose Christianity. The Spaniards then proceeded to the Inca capital of Cuzco and the destruction of Inca civilization began in earnest.

The leader of the Spanish conquest of Peru was Francisco Pizarro (*c.*1475-1541), a native of Extremadura like Cortez. He was middle-aged, a hard, silent man and another devout Catholic. The *Conquistadores*, as these men are called, saw themselves as continuing the *Reconquista* on a new and larger stage. When they cut down the Aztecs and Incas, the old *Reconquista* battle cry of 'Santiago!' was on their lips.

Catalonia
and Wilfrid the Hairy

Although Ferdinand and Isabella united Spain, they always saw it as a union of separate kingdoms, each with its own laws and customs. Isabella was queen of Castile and Ferdinand was king of Aragón and Navarre. Aragón was chiefly made up of Aragón itself, and of Valencia and Catalonia.

Catalonia had a proud, independent history, dating back to when Count Wilfrid the Hairy declared independence from southern France in the late 800s. Catalonians spoke, and speak, a language related to Spanish but separate from it. Catalan comes from an old French dialect called Langue d'Oc and is also spoken in Valencia. Ships from Catalonia and Aragón once ruled the eastern Mediterranean. The Catalan trading empire included Majorca, Minorca and Ibiza, all taken from the Moors by Aragonese kings in the thirteenth century.

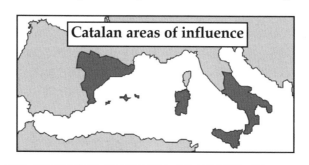

Catalan areas of influence

His mother was mad

Ferdinand died in 1516, twelve years after Isabella, supposedly of medication taken to improve his potency after remarrying to a young French princess.

The story of how his grandson Charles I came to inherit the Spanish crown is horribly complicated. It involves Charles's mother Juana *la Loca* (Juana 'the mad') who was Ferdinand and Isabella's daughter, and his father Philip the Handsome, briefly Philip I, who was a foreigner and a member of the Austrian royal family. The Austrian Hapsburgs were the most successful royal family in history and they achieved their success almost entirely by marrying people, Philip being no exception.

Suffice it to say that when Charles arrived in Spain in 1516, a tall youth with an absurdly large chin, known from that day to this as the 'Hapsburg Jaw', he could hardly mumble a word of Spanish. The Hapsburg family, chins and all, were to rule Spain for the next 130 years.

If you're in Tordesillas

Juana la Loca was Ferdinand and Isabella's daughter. She married Philip the Handsome in 1496 when she was twenty-six. Charles was the oldest of their several children. Juana became severely depressed after Philip the Handsome's death ten years later and took his coffin with her wherever she went, sometimes having it opened to check that he was still there. She was declared insane in 1509 and locked up in the Convent of Santa Clara in central Tordesillas, where she spent the next forty-six years, most of it in a windowless cell. The convent is open to the public.

> *Spain during the age of big chins can be divided into two unequal parts:*

Eighty-two years of super-power status.		Hundred and two years of decline.

> *Likewise the Hapsburg kings:*

Charles I (1516-56), brave and strong.
Philip II (1556-1598), dutiful.

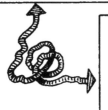

Philip III (1598-1621),
frivolous and feeble.
Philip IV (1621-65),
sex-mad and very feeble.
Charles II (1665-1700),
drooling mad and utterly feeble.

Seville and the Tower of Gold

It was during Charles I's reign that Spanish conquistadors, following in Columbus's footsteps, captured huge swathes of central and south America for the Spanish crown. What drove them was greed for gold and other precious metals. Between 1503 and 1560, it's estimated that *sixteen million* kilos of American silver were offloaded at the quayside in Seville to be weighed and counted in the Torre del Oro, the Tower of Gold - three times more than all the silver in Europe before that time. The silver came mainly from Mexico. By backing Columbus, Isabella had made a brilliant investment for her country.

You can have too much of a good thing. The Empire was rich but it was also very expensive to defend. All that money made people greedy. Swashbuckling freebooters

If you're in Seville
The Tower of Gold in Seville was built by the Arabs in 1220. It's still there and now it's a small naval museum, open to the public.

from northern Europe swarmed round the Spanish treasure fleets like bees round honey. Most of the treasure got through, but after that most of it also went to pay off the Italian and German bankers who financed Charles's wars - fought to protect his vast empire in the first place. Despite being the wealthiest country in Europe, Spain went as good as bankrupt several times over, in so far as countries *can* go bankrupt.

Charles abdicated from the Spanish throne in 1556, exhausted. Toothless and gout-ridden he holed up in the monastery of San Geronimo de Yuste in Extremadura with his collection of clocks, his pet cat and a parrot. His brother was given Germany to rule, whilst his only son Philip II got Spain, the Netherlands and the American colonies.

If you're in the Sierra de Gredos
The monastery of San Geronimo de Yuste is open to visitors. It's in the lovely, remote Sierra de Gredos hills, about 160 kilometres west of Madrid. It has a beautiful, peaceful garden with views of the hills beyond. Charles's private apartments are draped in black. You can see his sedan chair and his bed.

Madrid
And the king of papers

On 27 May 1527, the hot, stifling air in the palace at Valladolid hummed with the prayers of priests, like the buzzing of wasps. In a bedroom in the palace, deeply-religious Queen Isabella of Portugal, wife of Charles I, was giving birth. She hid her face beneath a sheet to hide the pain.

The new baby, Philip, grew up to be a sickly, serious child and deeply religious like his mother. As Philip II, he took over from his father at the age of twenty-nine, and for the next forty-two years he ruled his vast empire with an impressive sense of duty. Charles had fought battles; Philip II stayed home and signed papers. The whole business of empire ended up on his desk. He was like a spider at the centre of its web. He became known as *El Rey Papelero*, the king of official papers. They were prepared by an army of officials but he examined most of them personally, jotting remarks, issuing decrees, signing, amending, scratching out. It seemed incredible that his father had once called for pen and ink only to find that there was none in the palace.

The royal court moved from place to place and the papers and reports followed it across Spain in a chaotic paper chase, often being delivered to one palace soon after the court had moved on to the next. Philip decided to concentrate government in the small, central town of Madrid. He moved the capital there from Toledo in 1578. Over ten thousand officials moved too and Madrid doubled in size almost overnight.

Meanwhile Philip began work on a vast palace forty-eight

kilometres off, the Escorial, a huge, grey building, part palace and part monastery, which took twenty-two years to complete. Before it was completed, Philip had set up his office in a quiet room with a special window looking down on the chapel. On occasion he would watch the priests rehearse his own funeral and sometimes mass was celebrated round the clock.

If you're in Madrid

Part of the Palace of San Lorenzo de El Escorial is still used by the Spanish royal family but large parts of it are open to the public. It's named after the nearby village of Escorial and after San Lorenzo, a Christian martyr who was roasted alive on a griddle in Roman times. It's a huge place but Philip's rooms are simple. The bed where he died with its view of the church is still there.

Plateresque

Plateresque is a style of architecture unique to Spain, called after the swirling designs of silversmiths or 'plateros'. It flowered from around 1480 to 1540, slightly before the Escorial was built, a wonderful froth of shields and twisting shapes against smooth stone walls. It's a mixture of Europe and Islam, first created by Mudéjar architects. Mudéjars were Muslims living under Christian rule, as opposed to Mozárabes who were Christians living under Muslim rule. The ultimate example of plateresque is the façade of the ancient University of Salamanca, built around 1530.

Dutchmen, Englishmen and passionate poets

As a devout Catholic, Philip believed that Protestantism was a virus to be stamped out for the good of men's souls. He called Protestants 'heretics' and vowed 'never to rule over them', meaning that he would force them to convert. This posed a problem because Holland, one of the richest parts of the Spanish Empire, was overwhelmingly Protestant. His Dutch subjects were in a state of festering rebellion. Worse still, just over the water was England, the largest and most powerful of all Protestant states. English Protestants openly supported the Dutch. Adding injury to insult, English 'pirates' were a constant menace to the Spanish treasure fleets. These included 'pirates' such as Sir Francis Drake - one man's pirate is another man's hero.

Two years before he became King of Spain, Philip tried to solve the problem peacefully by marrying England's only Catholic monarch for years, Mary Tudor, eldest daughter of over-sized and many-wived Henry VIII, but that went down like a soggy balloon. The marriage was hugely unpopular in England, which ended up more Protestant than ever. Philip returned to Spain after just fourteen months, leaving Mary to face her disgruntled subjects alone. And Holland ended up in open rebellion. It declared its independence from Spain in 1581, partly due to English support and the war dribbled on until 1649.

In Brief - the Protestant problem

1568	Start of the Dutch revolt against Spanish/Hapsburg rule.
1581	Founding of the Dutch republic.
1585	Elizabeth I sends an English army to help the Dutch.
1587	The Pope declares a 'crusade' against England.
1588	Spain's 'Invincible Armada' sent to invade England.
1604	Spain and England make peace.

Armada

By 1586, Philip had had enough. He decided to crush the English once and for all and to put a tame, Catholic monarch on the English throne by force. Over the next two years, he gathered a fleet of 130 ships manned by 8,000 sailors and carrying around 19,000 soldiers. The plan was to meet up with with the Spanish army which was already in the the Netherlands and to escort it across the Channel to England.

Philip's 'Invincible Armada' set sail in May 1588. But the cards were stacked against the Spanish. The head of the Spanish expedition, the Duke of Medina Sidonia, was hopelessly seasick whereas the second-in-command of the English fleet was none other than that 'pirate' Sir Francis Drake, probably the greatest seaman of his age. The Spanish fleet was larger but the English ships were faster and their guns were longer range. The English harried the Spanish right the way up the Channel. Finally, off the coast of the Netherlands, English fireships broke up the Spanish fleet and a gale ripped through what was left. The sorry remnants fled back to Spain round the north coast of Scotland and Ireland.

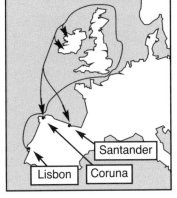

Among the soldiers on the Invincible Armada was a colourful, young playwright called Lope de Vega (1562-1635). Lope is the Shakespeare of Spain and Shakespeare's near-contemporary. He wrote over 1,400 plays and many other works. The plays are brilliantly witty and reflect Spanish society at the peak of its power.

The story of his love life, involving abductions, marriages, libel cases and temporary exile, is worth a large book in itself.

Turks and one-armed poets

The *Reconquista* had been won, but that was just in Spain. Elsewhere the Muslim Turkish Empire threatened all of southern and eastern Europe. It seemed to Philip that it was Spain's duty, as European superpower, to lead the fight against the Turks. In 1571, a Christian fleet under the command of Philip's dashing half-brother, Don Jon of Austria, crushed the Turkish fleet in the Gulf of Lepanto, off the Greek coast. More than four hundred war-galleys were involved in a vicious, confused battle. It was described by one of the fighters:

The sea foamed with blood, the bloody grave of dying bodies tossed by the waves ... the hail of arrows turned masts, yards and hulls into veritable hedgehogs or porcupines ... dying men swam for the galleys to save their lives even at the price of their freedom. They grabbed oars, rudders and ropes. Desperately they pleaded for mercy, only to have their hands sliced off ...

On board one of the Spanish galleys was a young soldier and up-coming writer called Miguel Cervantes. He'd been ordered to stay below decks because he was sick but had refused. During the course of the fighting he was badly wounded in his left hand. Cervantes, nicknamed *El Manco de Lepanto* (One-Handed of Lepanto), went on to become Spain's greatest ever writer. *El ingenioso hidalgo Don Quixote de la Mancha*, was his masterpiece.

Cervantes's life of adventure didn't end with the Battle of Lepanto. In 1575, while sailing home to Spain from Naples, where the Spanish fleet was based, he was captured by Muslim pirates from North Africa. He spent the next five years as a slave in Algiers. He led four escape attempts and was lucky not to be executed when each in turn was uncovered. In 1580, when his family finally managed to scrape together his ransom, he was on the point of being shipped for sale in the city of Istanbul (it was then called Constantinople) where he would probably have been lost for ever.

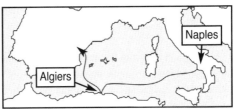

Safely back in Spain, he scraped a living as best he could, working at minor government jobs, such as buying supplies for the Armada. He moved house frequently and was imprisoned several times, usually for debt. In 1605, the year that the first volume of *Don Quixote* was published, his whole household were briefly locked up following a confused stabbing incident in Valladolid. He finally settled down in Madrid where he died in 1616.

If you're north of Madrid
Cervantes was born in Alcalá de Henares, about twenty kilometres northeast of Madrid. The address is Calle de la Imagen 2, in the old centre. The house has undergone major renovations and is now fully recreated as a seventeenth-century house. It's furnished with furniture from Cervantes's time along with other period items. It's open to the public as the *Museo Casa Natal de Miguel de Cervantes*.

SPAIN'S DARK SECRET
THE UNHOLY OFFICE

A bonfire in Seville

One hot afternoon in 1780, a woman stood in the main plaza in Seville, her hands tied with a length of rope. In her bound hands she carried a green cross, sign of those condemned to death by the Inquisition, the feared thought-police of old Spain. She wore a long, conical hat and beneath it a yellow robe called a *sanbenito*, standard wear for accused persons. The wood was piled high round the stake. The crowd in the stands were getting restless. It was time for the show to begin.

On this occasion, the crowd was denied the full excitement of a burning. The crime of the accused had been to claim supernatural powers, but at the last minute, she caved in and admitted that she'd made it up. She was let off.

In other words - she was strangled before the flames were lit beneath her.

That woman was one of the last victims of the Spanish Inquisition, set up in 1478 to root out all those who strayed from the true Catholic faith, or who had never been members of it in the first place.

> *Strangulation by garrotte was a common form of execution in Spain. Usually it took the form of an iron collar screwed to a post. The victim's neck was forced into the collar, which was then tightened by a screw. For portability, a wire with wooden handles could be used.*

Public punishments of those accused by the Inquisition were called *autos da fé* (acts of faith). They were a common event in Spain for hundreds of years. Towns would arrange for extra large *autos da fé* in honour of royal visits. The full ceremony, discontinued in 1790, combined elements of tedious church service, law court and brutal violence. Stands were erected, usually in a plaza, and the public came from miles around. On the appointed date, the accused, dressed in conical hats and sanbenitos, were paraded before the crowd while priests read out the charges. Then the accused were either forgiven and received lesser punishments - or were kept by for burning. The ceremony, including the burnings, could take all day, although the burnings might take place later.

If you're in Madrid

The Plaza Major, just off the Calle Major in central Madrid, was the scene of some of the grandest *autos da fé*. It was specially designed for major public events and was lined with balconies for good viewing. Royals and top officials sat within earshot of the groans of the victims. At an *auto da fé* in 1680 in honour of his new bride, Charles II lit the first brand.

The Black Legend
And an unnatural end in Córdoba

All European countries were once horribly intolerant. It's just that Spain kept on being intolerant for longer than most. Public burnings went on until the late eighteenth century. The Inquisition itself wasn't permanently abolished until 1834. Even as late as the 1960s, Jewish synagogues and Protestant churches were forbidden to display any religious symbols on their outside walls.

The *Leyenda Negra*, the Black Legend of Spanish cruelty and intolerance, also lasted a long time and it still annoys the Spanish. It took root in the sixteenth century and was fuelled by the mysterious death of Philip II's son Carlos in 1568.

Carlos was inbred. He had Juana *la Loca*, The Crazy One, for grandmother through both his father and mother who were first cousins. He had a small body, a huge head, a vile temper, a stammer and a cruel streak. He attempted at least six murders and in 1562 he smashed his head open while chasing the pretty daughter of a servant through the palace, at full gallop so to speak. Eventually Philip had him locked up in the Alcázar in Córdoba and there Carlos inconveniently died. Philip was widely (and probably unfairly) suspected of having had his son murdered. His supposed crime was used by Protestants in England and the Netherlands to help spread the Black Legend of Spanish nastiness.

Getting Inquisitive
Christian Spain has always been a very religious country, at least until recently, since it grew out of the *Reconquista* of

the Muslim south, a religious war. Isabella of Castile was typically devout. Although a fundamentally decent person, on her deathbed she begged that her husband Ferdinand would:

> *... give himself unremittingly to the conquest of Africa and the war for the Faith against the Moors.*

It was Isabella who set up the Spanish Inquisition or 'Holy Office' back in 1478 to stamp out non-believers in Castile. There had been other inquisitions before and in other countries but her Inquisition turned out to be a monster. It lasted for over three hundred years and at its peak it had over 20,000 agents. Spain began to suffocate under a vile climate of fear and suspicion. The job of the agents was to sniff out Protestants, Jews and Muslims, often using horrible tortures to make victims confess. The Inquisition also controlled what books Spanish people were allowed to read. Isabella's personal confessor Tomás de Torquemada became Grand Inquisitor in 1483. He was responsible for the deaths of around 2,000 people and over 100,000 trials.

If you're in Santillana del Mar

There's a small Museum of the Inquisition in Santillana del Mar, near the Plaza del Canton in the centre of town. It has over eighty gruesome exhibits, some extremely odd and unpleasant. The inquisitors were imaginative as well as unbelievably cruel. There's a full scale guillotine in the garden.

Jews, *Conversos* and *Marranos*

By 1492, Jews had lived in Spain for 1,500 years. They'd done well. They were part of the country - almost.

The Muslims were fairly tolerant of Jews, as had been a good number of Christians. Peter the Cruel, (or 'the Just' depending on your point of view), King of Castile 1350-69, appointed Jews to the highest positions in the land.

But many other Christians were intolerant. Jews were persecuted and expelled by the Visigoths in the 700s and there were some nasty massacres during the Middle Ages, especially after the death of Peter the Cruel, killed by his half brother Henry Trastamara in a savage hand-to-hand fight. As Henry plunged his dagger into his brother's heart, he's said to have cursed him - 'You bastard Jew!'.

The worst of the massacres came in 1391. In June of that year, the Christians of Seville turned on their Jewish neighbours and massacred 4,000 of them. The trouble spread to Córdoba where the dead were piled in heaps, and from there right across Spain. The riots and the massacres lasted three months.

Bad feeling towards the Jews, who were often rich and successful, had been growing for years. As a result of these horrors, up to a third of the Jewish population chose to convert to Christianity. They became known as 'New Christians' or *Conversos*. As *Conversos* they could operate freely and were less likely to be massacred when things got rough. But they were never completely safe. Conversos were suspected of being *Marranos* - Jewish in secret. *Marrano* originally meant a 'swine'. Conversion seemed too convenient to suspicious minds: your local wealthy merchant or tax collector was a Jew, the next day he became a Christian and had a bit of holy water sprinkled on him and bingo - he was as good as you were. Anti-Jewish feeling got worse as the years went by.

Finally, in 1492 less than three months after the capture of Granada, Ferdinand and Isabella ordered the expulsion of all Jews from Spain. More than half of them left. The rest became *Conversos*, or perhaps even *Marranos*.

Moriscos
A different sort of bonfire in Granada
In 1492, after the Jews had been expelled, the conquered Muslims of Granada were allowed to remain Muslim at first. They were, however, offered money to convert and many did - so many that it was almost an industrial process. At one mass christening in the late 1490s, the holy water was sprinkled on their heads from a vast, swirling mop-like construction. Converted Muslims were called

Moriscos. *Moriscos* were feared almost as much as Muslims and Jews. There was a large population of them, especially in the south. They were seen as a threat. As one disgruntled old Christian put it:

> *They are Spain's treasure chest, its magpies, its weasels. Whatever they get hold of they either devour or hide away ... neither men nor women enter convents or monasteries, but they all marry and multiply.*

The real trouble was that the *Moriscos* kept to their old ways, speaking Arabic and wearing their traditional clothing. They refused to stop bathing on a regular basis and they were hard working. They might as well have stayed Muslim for all the difference it seemed to make.

Gradually the noose tightened. In 1499, Isabella's fanatical Archbishop Jiménez de Cisneros ordered all Arabic religious books to be burnt in a huge bonfire in the centre of Granada. Thousands of unique treasures went up in smoke. Then, in 1502, *all* Muslims were forced to convert - or else leave Spain for good. And in the last sad act (1609-11), all the *Moriscos* were forced to leave, converted or not.

Pure blood

It was definitely best not to be Jewish or Muslim if you wanted to get on in Spain after 1492. In fact, it was best not to have any Jewish or Muslim ancestors of any kind. *Limpieza de sangre* ('purity of blood') became a national obsession. People of mixed race lived in fear of professional investigators, called *linajudos*, who made it their business to ferret out 'inaccuracies' in family trees. Jobs could be barred to those who could not prove pure Spanish descent. In 1546, the Archbishop of Toledo remarked that no one would buy a horse without knowing its pedigree so why should he appoint a potential enemy to high office if he didn't know his bloodline?

Limpieza de sangre was especially a problem for aristocrats because on the whole they could trace their ancestors further back than common people. As a result, they were more likely to have inconvenient forebears available for discovery by the *linajudos*.

BASKET CASE
WHAT WENT WRONG

They ate pot

Sixteenth and seventeenth-century Spaniards were obsessed by class. At the top were a handful of aristocrats who owned 97% of the land of Castile, plus large chunks elsewhere. One earlier aristocrat, Leónor de Albuquerque, had been able to travel right across Spain without once stepping off her own land. Aristocratic behaviour was often as 'un-Spanish' as their blood. Hundreds of years of living next door to Muslims had left its mark. Aristocratic families in Spain tended to keep their women hidden away indoors. In their graceful, private rooms, upper class Spanish women might sit Arab-fashion, on cushions rather than chairs, and they had a weird habit of nibbling little bits of glazed pottery, a North African custom.

Next down the social ladder after the aristocrats came the *hidalgos* - minor gentry. Because the aristocrats had so much land, many hidalgos had no land at all.

But the hidalgos had their pride. Hidalgos didn't pay tax, they couldn't be sentenced to be rowing-slaves on the

Mediterranean galleys or to be tortured - and they could stick *Don* ('Sir') in front of their surnames, as in *Don Quixote*, showing that they were superior to lesser mortals. Don Quixote is in many ways a typical hidalgo, brave, proud and penniless. Miguel de Cervantes came from a hidalgo family so he knew what he was talking about. Once, to prove that the Cervantes family were hidalgos, a witness testified that he'd seen Miguel and his brothers jousting - and that he'd never seen them pay any tax.

Jousting and not paying tax were what counted.

Hidalgo check list

Look good, even if you can only afford to show your face in your home town once a year. Appearance is everything.

Never ever engage in any form of manual labour.

Never pay any tax.

The work allergy

Manual labour was social suicide for hidalgos. The kiss of death. A life of poverty was preferable and was often their fate. To try to help them, in 1773 a law was passed declaring that trades such as cobbler, carpenter and tailor were 'honourable' and therefore okay, but it made no difference. The culture was too strong. For several hundred years, Spain suffered from the opposite of a work ethic. The idea was to live off your wits and never get your hands dirty.

Gambling offered the chance to make money without working so was very much to hidalgo taste, coming a close fourth to women, clothes and horses. Gambling establishments stayed open twenty-four hours a day.

Sometimes there were toilets in the gaming rooms so that players could stay at play while their luck was in.

Spain was crippled. The hidalgos couldn't or wouldn't work and in some places there were as many hidalgos as there were tax payers. It was hardly surprising that the government kept going bankrupt. To cap it all, during the 1600s the stream of treasure from America dried to a trickle and Spain suffered from rampant inflation. Even farming ran into problems. Big landlords owned the vast, migratory flocks of sheep of the Mesta, and sheep and crops didn't mix. A law of 1501 stated that land once grazed by the Mesta could never be used for any other purpose. This was scarcely a recipe for progress.

If you're driving across Extremadura
If you've got wheels and you're driving across Extremadura or Castile you may notice wide, grassy tracks which are either cut by the road or run beside it. These are the ancient drove roads of the Mesta. There were once around 124,000 kilometres of them. The biggest, the *cañadas reales*, are over seventy metres across.

The economy was crippled and even people's thinking processes were crippled by conservatism brought on by the Inquisition. In the mid 1600s there was a plan to link the rivers Manzanares and Tagus by a navigable canal. Hostile witnesses at the official enquiry claimed that if God had meant the rivers to be navigable he would have arranged it himself!

Don Juan

The odd thing is that while Spain went from bad to worse financially, it blossomed culturally. There was *Don Quixote* of course, first volume published 1605. And there were countless poems and plays. Theatre was pop culture as it was elsewhere in Europe during the same period - this was the era of Shakespeare. (Interestingly, Cervantes and Shakespeare died on the same day in 1616.) Teams of travelling players moved from town to town, setting up stages in inn yards or public plazas. The inns were colourful places. Guests ate together at a long table with one communal knife chained to the middle of it. Apart from plays, there might be public readings or dancing to the guitar. Cervantes described one such troupe of players:

All their baggage could have fitted in one sack. It consisted of four white sheepskins, embellished with gilded leather, four false beards and wigs, and four shepherds' crooks.

Women's experience of public social occasions could be rather fraught. Actresses would lock themselves up between performances so as to avoid being pestered. Women in the audience sat in an area called the 'stewing pan', often partitioned off to give a little privacy. Don Juan was a reality long before he was written about, in 1630 in a play called *The Deceiver of Seville*, by Tirso de Molina (1584-1648), one of the greatest Spanish playwrights.

The Deceiver of Seville is the first and best of all 'Don Juan' plays. Don Juan lies and cheats to get his wicked way and then discards his female victims like worn out socks. He's oversexed and has absolutely no conscience at all. There were many real-life Don Juans in Spanish history to base the character on, including Don Juan de Mañara, the original. On de Mañara's tomb in Seville are the proud words:

Here lie the ashes of the greatest sinner who ever lived.

The end of the Hapsburgs

The last Hapsburgs lived lives of gloomy royal ceremony in their stifling palaces. Due to inbreeding, they became feebler with each generation. Philip IV (reigned 1621-50), the second to last, was pleasure-loving and ineffectual. He was painted by the artist Velázquez (1599-1660) who caught the Hapsburg chin and the dull face to perfection. Velázquez also painted the stuffy royal court, dark and brooding with its fashionable dwarfs. Philip IV loved the work of Velázquez and had all other pictures of himself removed from the palace walls.

After Philip IV came Charles II, 'the Bewitched' (1661-1700), last of the Hapsburgs. Charles II was worse than feeble. He was king from the age of four but couldn't sit up till he was six. He was barely able to wipe his own bottom (figuratively speaking) let alone lead a major European country.

During his long reign, Spain hit rock bottom. By the time he died, it was weak and almost defenceless. Powerful countries got ready to fight over the remains. The war which followed was called the War of the Spanish Succession (1701-14).

And when the fighting finished - there was a French Bourbon king sitting on the Spanish throne.

> *The Treaty of Utrecht which ended the War of the Spanish Succession was how Britain acquired Gibraltar. It was a concession extracted from Spain while Spain was weak, and British possession of Gibraltar is still a bone of contention between the two countries.*

BOURBONS
THEY ABOLISHED THE PYRENEES

Madrid and the giant clippers

Sunday 23 March 1766 was a bad day for Madrid. There was much muttering outside the churches. A new law had been passed to control men's clothing. At that time, standard wear for all Spanish males was the traditional long cape and broad-brimmed hat. Now the government had gone and banned them. Anyone who ignored the new law was grabbed in the street and their cloak and hat were clipped to the right size with specially designed, extra-large clippers. The men of Madrid were understandably annoyed.

At that time, Madrid was suffering from a crime wave and the government was determined to stamp it out. The banning of the long, traditional cape was one of several anti-crime measures. Already, cafes were allowed only one entrance so that criminals couldn't escape through the back door. The long cape had made it too easy for thieves to hide their ill-gotten gains. The new look was to be a short cape and the French tricorn hat.

Or possibly not. That afternoon and evening, a furious

mob raced through the streets, tore down the streetlights, sacked the palace of the chief minister and forced King Charles III himself to flee the capital. Next day he cancelled the new law.

> *The long cape went out of fashion later, when the government cunningly made it the official uniform of the public executioner.*

Bourbons

Despite the 'cloak and hat' law, Charles III was a good king who tried to modernise Spain. His problem was that most of Spain didn't want to be modernised. It certainly didn't want to be modernised by a foreigner, and especially not a foreigner like Charles, who was French and a Bourbon to boot.

The Bourbons in Spain	
Philip V	reigned 1700-46
Ferdinand VI	reigned 1746-59
Charles III	reigned 1759-88
Charles IV	reigned 1788-1808
Napoleonic Wars	
Ferdinand VII	reigned 1813-33
Isabella II	reigned 1833-68
Alfonso XII	reigned 1874- 85
Alfonso XIII	reigned 1886-1941

Modernisation was unpopular, but Charles was a determined man and he persisted. The story of Spain in the eighteenth century is that of a country dragged moaning and kicking into the modern world, long after everyone else in western Europe.

Abolishing the Pyrenees

If only Spain could have had more rulers like Charles III, it might have avoided a lot of suffering later. But the other Bourbons didn't have his ability. The first of them, also the worst, was Philip V, a manic-depressive who swung between extremes of mood. Either he spent weeks in bed without shaving or changing his stinking clothes, or else the palace echoed to scenes of wild romping as the king and his royal dwarves chased the queen and her attendants from room to room through the royal apartments.

Back in 1700, when Philip V first accepted the crown of Spain for the Bourbons, his grandfather, the French king Louis XIV, who was extremely pleased, said:

We have abolished the Pyrenees.

Back then it seemed that at last Spain was going to open

up to the outside world. The Bourbon rulers, their foreign advisers and Spanish supporters were all eager for the fresh air of new ideas. But against them was old Spain, the dead hand of the big aristocrats, the Mesta, the proud hidalgos - and especially the Catholic Church.

By 1788, there were 200,000 priests, monks and nuns in the country, one for every fifty Spaniards. There were 2,000 monasteries and 1,000 convents as well as countless churches of all shapes and sizes.The church was against all things liberal, meaning, at that time, freemasonry, atheism, Protestantism and in fact change of almost any kind. And it was still powerful. The last public burning by the Inquisition in 1780 was frighteningly medieval for the date, and the Inquisition wasn't abolished until 1834. The universities too were a throwback to the past because they were dominated by the clergy. In other parts of Europe, science was making great strides; in Spain, students still argued over subjects such as: 'What language is spoken by angels?'

Some advice on how to walk
And whether to wear glasses
At the heart of eighteenth-century Spain was Madrid, now well-established as the capital city. Like Spain itself, it was half way between Europe and Africa. Houses faced inwards. Windows onto the street were covered in metal gratings and girls were closely guarded. If a young man went courting, he had to speak to his girl through the grating. It was called 'eating the iron'. There were no pavements until the 1760s and the streets were lit by smoky oil lamps.

Dirty, dark and dangerous it might have been, but eighteenth-century Madrid hummed with life and must have been a wonderfully exotic place. Rich dandies called *petimetres* prowled the streets. Your typical petimetre wore a coat with vast buttons, extra-tight breeches, silk stockings and a red, floral waistcoat with several other waistcoats jutting underneath. His enormous cravat was tied so tightly that his eyes bulged and his face went purple. There were other exotic creatures. The *currutaco* was a later version of the petimetre. A journal advised the currutacos on how to walk:

Practise in front of a mirror two hours a day with fetters tied to your feet.

Steps must be long and springy when the fetters come off.

The head must move from side to side and the eyes wander at all times, as if distracted.

Out on the street, the currutaco dashed through the crowds with head swinging, his chest stuck out like a pigeon and with his elbows jutting like wings, so as to make people get out of the way.

The female version of the petimetre was the *petimetra*. Female fashions were as extreme as the male. In the 1780s, glasses were all the rage. Young girls with perfect vision walked around with their faces hidden behind huge, phoney pairs of specs.

Macho

It may seem odd to dwell so long on obscure eighteenth century dandies, but there's a point to it. On his head the petimetre wore a French-style tricorn hat, not the traditional Spanish broad-brimmed hat. The very word petimetre came from the French *petit maître* meaning 'little master'. Petimetres came from rich families and followed the latest French fashions and ideas. Because of this they were scorned by the *majos*, working class dandies. Majos clung to the long cape, wore their long hair in hairnets, just as El Cid had worn his beard centuries before, and smoked huge, black cigars, considered thoroughly antisocial by the upper classes. They even cultivated the good old odour of sanctity. Any majo who changed his underwear more than once a week was thought to be a wimp - resulting skin diseases were said to be a problem.

Majos were tough. They never went out without at least a folding knife hidden in their sashes. Their girlfriends, the *majas*, wore low-cut dresses and lace shawls called mantillas. They could be as tough as their boyfriends and they too often carried daggers - in their left garters. Majas had more freedom than the bespectacled petimetras.

The Swoon

Upper class petimetres tended to steer clear of the majos for understandable reasons, but along with most of young, eighteenth-century Madrid, they couldn't resist visiting lower class dances which were so much more fun than stuffy, upper class balls. Lower class dances were candlelit affairs where the majos and majas strutted their stuff through the long, hot nights to the seductive strumming of guitars. The Spanish guitar had changed gradually since the 1600s - it waited till the eighteenth century to get its sixth string - but it's a genuinely Spanish invention or the majos wouldn't have liked it.

The most popular dances were stately *seguidillas*, *fandangos* - harmonious convulsion of the entire body - and *contradanzas*, said by some to come from the English 'country dances' although more likely it came from the French words *contre dance* - 'dance against' - because the dancers formed lines facing each other.

The *desmayo* ('swoon') was an especially scandalous contradanza.

The *meona* was a contradanza in which everyone filled their mouths with water and squirted it into the centre of the circle of dancers at the climax.

Flamenco

Flamenco is Andalusian gypsy music and dance which took on its present form in the eighteenth century. Gypsies are thought to have migrated from India to Europe during the Middle Ages. Once in southern Spain, their music was influenced by Spanish popular music such as the fandango and by the music of the Spanish Muslims and Jews. Oddly, Flamenco is also a Spanish word for Flemish (Belgian), due to a mistaken notion that Belgians were gypsy-like.

Bull fights

Majos were for all things Spanish and against all things foreign. Foreigners were sissy. So were upper-class Spaniards with their less-than-pure blood and their mincing ways. And what could be more Spanish than a bullfight? Bullfights go back all the way to the Roman Empire and before. There are paintings of bulls on the caves at Altamira, so perhaps bullfighting goes back as far as that.

For centuries bullfighting had been an aristocratic hobby. Upper-class young men on horseback had killed the bulls with lances. Now, in the late eighteenth century, bullfighting became mass, popular entertainment and the killing was done by *matadors*, full-time professionals from working class backgrounds who performed for money, on foot and with swords, as they still do nowadays.

Over the next hundred years bullfighting became big business. Bullrings were built by businessmen as business ventures, purely to make money, although bullfights were also staged as charitable, fundraising exercises by local bigwigs. The first bullrings were modelled on the town squares where bullfights were traditionally staged, but the bulls tended to cower in the corners so the round design of today was developed.

> *The Spanish 'stand' at the Paris International Exposition of 1889 was a bullring with electric lighting and a retractable roof. The organisers hoped to turn bullfighting into an export industry.*

Matadors became professional, sporting celebrities, the best of them becoming cult figures. By the 1880s a top matador could earn more in an afternoon than a schoolteacher could earn in a year. Little statues of them were sold, their faces were embroidered on handkerchiefs. They even endorsed commercial products.

If you're in Seville
The oldest purpose-built bullring in Spain is the Plaza de Toros de la Maestranza, by the banks of the Guadalquivir in Seville, completed in 1763. It has a beautiful circle of arches. Here and at Ronda is where the modern style of bullfighting on foot began.

The case against
Not all Spanish people have been in favour of bullfighting. Many have disapproved, and still do. Back in 1495, Queen Isabella, admittedly appalled by the number of men who died rather than the suffering of the bulls, suggested that the bulls' horns should be wrapped in leather, but in the interests of fair play her suggestion was ignored. In 1597,

bullfighting was banned by the Pope but with a similar lack of success. In the nineteenth century, humane societies campaigned against the sport. There were criticisms of the effect of matadors tightly swathed buttocks on impressionable young ladies:

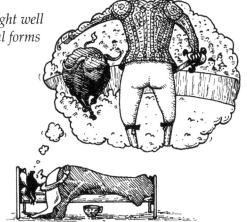

A maiden's cheek might well redden at the graceful forms of the strong young men, with their sinew welling round and fair beneath the tight jackets of satin, the coloured pantaloons and the silken hose.

Revolutionary wars

Good, punctual Charles III died in 1788, a year before the start of the French Revolution. Things might have turned out differently for Spain if he'd stayed alive a little longer. His son, Charles IV, was a useless slob whose favourite activities were eating huge meals and hunting. He left day to day business to his wife's lover, Manuel de Godoy who, strangely, was a close friend.

It was the worst possible time for Spain to have a lazy slob for a king. Europe in the period of the French Revolution was a dangerous place. Powerful countries such as Britain, Russia and the north-German kingdom of Prussia were competing with France for dominance. Due to the incompetence of Charles IV and Godoy, Spain got embroiled in war with revolutionary France and French troops occupied the north of the country.

In March 1808, almost forty-two years to the day since the revolt of the giant clippers, the mob rose again, this time at Aranjuez to the south of Madrid, where the court was then in residence. As usual, the rioters were against things foreign but this time they were rioting about something a lot more important than the length of the national cloak. Their country had been humiliated by the French invasion. Manuel de Godoy was to blame and they wanted his blood.

Once again the house of the chief minister was trashed. Godoy barely escaped with his life. He had to hide for thirty-six hours in some rolled up matting in the attic of his mansion in order to avoid being slaughtered. To save Godoy's skin, Charles IV, was forced to abdicate in favour of his son, the equally slobbish Ferdinand VII.

But then, within a few weeks, Charles changed his mind and decided he wanted his crown back. He turned to the French leader Napoleon for help. The whole hopeless family - Charles, his toothless, over-sexed wife Maria Luisa, their son Ferdinand and the hapless Godoy - met Napoleon at Bayonne in France to ask him to sort things out.

Which is exactly what Napoleon did - he put his brother Joseph on the throne instead. Charles and Maria Luisa were exiled to Rome and Ferdinand was given a house to live in in Valencay in France.

CADIZ GETS CONSTITUTIONAL
THE NINETEENTH CENTURY

Sideburns in Madrid

On 18 May 1814, an ugly man with long, dark sideburns rode into Madrid on a white charger to shouts of ecstatic welcome from the crowd. Ferdinand VII, nastiest of all the Bourbons, was back and the Spanish people greeted their new master like a conquering hero, even though he'd been invited back by the French enemy, by Napoleon of all people. For the past six years, Napoleon had been keeping Ferdinand in pampered exile in France in case he became useful later, which he now had.

As far as the crowd was concerned, anything was better than Joseph Bonaparte. Spanish people, all except a minority, had loathed Joseph and loathed the French occupying forces who'd come with him. They'd been fighting like tigers to remove them ever since they arrived. Poor Joseph. When Napoleon handed him the crown of Spain back in 1808, he was handing him a poisoned chalice. Joseph was a decent chap, far more decent than Ferdinand, but his five-year reign, if you could call it that, had been a nightmare.

Joe Bottles

Pepe Botella (Joe Bottles), as Joseph was rather unfairly called by his subjects due to his rumoured fondness for alchoholic beverages, had come to Spain with the best of intentions. He'd wanted to modernise it. But the majority of the Spanish people, all except some liberals, didn't want to be modernised. They wanted him out. Their 'War of Independence' against the French was the cruellest of all the cruel conflicts of the Napoleonic Wars. The Spanish rebels had no regular army so they used guerrilla tactics - *guerilla* means 'little war'. After several years of savage bloodshed, they succeeded. The French were driven out by a combination of Spanish guerrillas and the regular British army under General Wellington, in a conflict known in Britain as the 'Peninsular War'.

Dos de Mayo

The Spanish first rose against the French on 2 May 1808 - *Dos de Mayo* ('Second of May') as it's called in Spanish history books. This happened almost as soon as Joseph became king. Peasants from the surrounding countryside filtered into town armed with pitchforks, blunderbusses and whatever else they could lay their hands on. When night fell, they slit the throats of any of Joseph's French soldiers who were out in the streets and then disembowelled them. The French reacted ruthlessly. Within a month all of Spain was in flames.

Dos de Mayo, or rather the execution of the rebels by French soldiers afterwards, was painted by the artist Francisco Goya, then already sixty-two years old. For thirty years he'd lived the comfortable life of a fashionable artist and official painter to the royal court. Now the brush which had painted genteel ladies and gentlemen began to paint the horrors of war. The titles of his anti-war paintings say it all: *Shouting's No Good*, *Do They Belong to Another Race?* (of starving women and children), *He Deserved It* (of a wounded French soldier about to be lynched). It was indeed a brutal conflict.

Cádiz

All the while that the War of Independence raged, Spain had no proper central government. Leadership was down to local juntas. Spain was effectively a republic because it had no king - Ferdinand had been ousted by Napoleon and Joseph was one of the enemy. This gave Spanish liberals their chance to modernise the country. At a meeting in Cádiz in 1812, they drew up a new constitution. The *Constitution of Cádiz* called for a united Spain, constitutional monarchy as in Britain, and an elected parliament or *Cortes*.

By 1812, the French were losing the war in Spain and they needed a way out. This was when Napoleon realised that the obnoxious Ferdinand might be useful after all. He decided to ask Ferdinand to come back on the basis of a new constitution, as a constitutional monarch with an elected parliament. The idea was that Joseph's modernising efforts would continue under new management.

Ferdinand was a selfish, unimaginative toad, one of the worst kings Spain had been cursed with since the 1600s. As soon as he returned in 1814, he revoked the constitution and dissolved the parliament. Twelve thousand liberals were sent into exile.

Sadly, Ferdinand had plenty of support - the usual culprits: aristocracy, die-hard nationalists and the church. The church was still a force to be reckoned with and it wasn't shy about taking sides. For most of the nineteenth century, Spanish children were asked in their catechism:

What sin is committed by him who votes liberal?

To which the answer was:

Generally a mortal sin.

The end of the Spanish Empire
The Napoleonic Wars finished off the Spanish Empire. Spain under Joseph was an ally of France and therefore an enemy of Britain. To weaken Spain, the Royal Navy cut all sea links between Spain and her American colonies.

Cut off from the mother country, the Spanish colonies of Latin America began to trade with the United States. This trade was more profitable than their trade with Spain had been. It became obvious that they would make more money if they *stayed* independent of Spain once the war was over.

The Napoleonic Wars ended in 1815 when Napoleon was defeated at the Battle of Waterloo by the British and their allies. By that time of course, Ferdinand VII was back on the Spanish throne and, Ferdinand being Ferdinand, he wasn't going to give the Spanish-American colonies their independence. With royal support, Spanish armies and loyal colonists fought savagely to re-establish Spanish control - but failed. The territory which was to become Argentina declared independence in 1816. Further north, a brilliant Venezuelan called Simon Bolivar led a War of Independence (1808-1826) and won. Most of the countries of modern South America emerged from the chaos of this war and Bolivia is named after Simon Bolivar out of gratitude for his achievement.

Much the same thing happened in Central America, although in Mexico the first freedom fighters were native Mexicans and mixed race *mestizos* rather than aristocratic *creoles*, colonists of pure Spanish blood. Led by a priest, the native Mexicans rose in savage revolt in 1810. The revolt was first crushed and then taken over by local creoles who went on to lead the fight for independence. Mexico declared its independence in 1822 and the rest of Central America soon followed.

Carlistas
The nineteenth century dragged on and Spain continued to have problems. Ferdinand was a backward-looking oaf, but he wasn't backward-looking enough for some people. A section of the population was determined to drag the country right back to the Middle Ages, or something approaching it. These people turned to Ferdinand's

younger brother, Don Carlos, for leadership. They became known as *Carlistas*.

When Ferdinand died in 1833, family members punched each other over the deathbed, Carlos and his supporters on one side, the rest of the family on the other. The blows then developed into gunshots and the Carlistas fought a seven-year civil war (1833-40) against supporters of Ferdinand's three-year-old daughter Isabella, who was the rightful heir to the throne. Isabella was backed by liberals calling for modernization. They were terrified of what Carlos would do to the country - and to them.

> *There were three Carlist wars against the liberals: 1833-40, in the 1850s and in the 1870s. The keenest of the Carlistas were the Basques who believed that Carlos would give them back their ancient, independent rights and privileges.*

'That woman'
Nineteenth century Britain had Queen Victoria; Spain had Isabella II. What a contrast! Victoria was tiny; Isabella was vast once she grew up. Victoria was prim; Isabella loved to dance - hippopotamus-like cavorting which was less than pleasing to the eye. Unlike Victoria, Isabella was an embarrassment to her subjects. They called her *esa señora* - 'that woman'.

Highly sexed like many Bourbons before her, Isabella was married off to a cousin at the very beginning of her reign. 'If we don't hurry, the heir will arrive before the husband', said the courtiers.

Cousin Francisco of Assisi, husband-to-be, was a mousy youth with a high-pitched voice. He was given the nickname *Paquito*. 'I'll marry him if he's a man' Isabella is reported to have remarked. Paquito never really believed that her first child was his.

Isabella reigned for thirty-five years, thirty-five years of gargantuan galumphing in the palace, too many chocolates and endless scandals involving her courtiers and relatives.

In 1854, the queen mum had to flee the country due to financial hanky panky over railway contracts (Spain was modernising despite itself). By 1868, nearly everyone had had enough. There was a military coup and Isabella was forced to leave the country.

The First Republic
A general called Juan Prim led the military coup against Isabella and took over the government. He was a liberal so he looked round for a nice, liberal king to replace her. Above all, he wanted nineteenth-century Spain to keep modernising - and he wanted to keep out the Carlistas. In fact, he wanted a constitutional monarchy, somewhat along the lines of the British monarchy. No easy task. Prim is reported to have said:

Looking for a democratic king in Europe is like looking for an atheist in heaven.

After scouring the palaces of Europe, a young Italian prince called Amadeo was eventually chosen. Poor Amadeo. Immediately he set foot in Spain he found himself plunged into Spain's ruthless, unforgiving struggle between liberals and traditionalists. On the day Amadeo arrived, Prim was assassinated.

Amadeo resigned in February 1873 after reigning for two impossible years. Now finally Spain became a republic, the First Republic. It seemed to many that a new dawn had at last arisen. Now the Liberals would be able to put in place the reforms which the country so desperately needed.

Or would they? The First Republic lasted just over a year and was a disaster. No one could agree about anything. There was war with the Carlistas in the north and regional revolts in the south. Anarchy beckoned. By December 1874, most people had had enough, and Spain went back to being a monarchy. Isabella's son Alfonso, a student at the famous British military academy at Sandhurst, was invited to be the new king - Alfonso XII.

A pregnant possibility

All's well that ends well. Except that in nineteenth-century Spain it very rarely did. After a brief period of peace and prosperity, Alfonso died (1885), aged only twenty-seven at which time his young wife was pregnant with their only son. The next king, Alfonso XIII, became king before he was born, so to speak. As a result, he was doted on by his mother and fawned on by courtiers from earliest infancy.

Poor Spain. Alfonso XIII never really had a chance. His only real passion was the army and to a lesser extent the Catholic Church, a limited set of interests with which to see in the twentieth century. He began to rule personally in 1902 when aged only sixteen, and he was forced to leave the country in 1931, twenty-nine years and thirty-three hopeless governments later.

The Black Year

Most Spanish colonies broke free from the Spanish Empire back in the early 1800s, but in 1898 there were still some colonies left. The Spanish-American War of that year was the final disaster. Spain lost two naval battles then sued for peace. Cuba became independent and the USA acquired Guam, Puerto Rico and the Philippines. The Spanish Empire was reduced to a few outposts in North Africa.

In Brief - the Nineteenth Century

1808	French invade - start of War of Independence.
1810	American colonies start to break free.
1812	Constitution of Cádiz.
1814	Return of Ferdinand VII.
1825	By now, most colonies have won their independence from Spain.
1833-40	First Carlist War.
1833-68	Reign of Isabella II
1834	Inquisition abolished during a liberal interlude.
1868	General Prim and the army take over.
1870-3	Short reign of Amadeo of Savoy.
1873-4	First Republic.
1874-85	Reign of Alfonso XII, son of Isabella.
1885	Accession of Alfonso XIII.
1898	Spanish-American War - last big colonies lost.

THE SECOND REPUBLIC
REASONS NOT TO DANCE
WITH DEAD NUNS

Taking sides

By 1900, and during the entire reign of Alfonso XIII, Spanish attitudes were fixed in stone:

> *On the left:*
> republicans, liberals, socialists, anarchists and communists

> *On the right:*
> monarchists, the army and the church.

On my right

In the first part of nineteenth century, the Catholic Church was central to the right wing way of seeing things. Most right-wingers believed passionately that Spain was a Catholic country or it was nothing. The Church was still powerful into the twentieth century. Even into the 1930s, Catholics were supposed not to eat with Protestants on pain of excommunication, and the bodies of Protestants

IS THAT A PROTESTANT FOOT? DON'T TOUCH IT!

could be refused burial in Spanish soil - except on beaches at low tide. Churchmen weren't shy about making their political opinions known. As late as 1931, the Archbishop of Toledo referred to republicans as 'enemies of the Kingdom of Jesus Christ'.

And on my left ...

Since the Church was against the left, it was hardly surprising that the left, and especially left-wing extremists, was against the Church. There were plenty of left-wing extremists: socialists, syndicalists, various types of communists and anarchists.

Especially anarchists. Spanish anarchists had a long history of extremism. They shot dead two prime ministers (1897 and 1912) and indulged in some very unpleasant rioting. In 1909 in Barcelona, anarchist rioters burned twenty-two churches and thirty-four convents. They removed the dried-up bodies of long-dead nuns from their burial spots in the convents and displayed them on the pavements outside. To show their contempt for the Church, some drunken rioters pretended to dance with the corpses.

General Primo

By the 1920s, most Spanish people, and not just left wingers, were heartily tired of Alfonso XIII. Alfonso had started off trying to rule through parliament but took more and more power into his own hands as the years went by. In 1921 a Spanish army in Morocco, then an unruly Spanish protectorate, was massacred by Moroccan tribesmen. A parliamentary report placed the blame squarely on Alfonso's shoulders and he was ousted by a patriotic general called Miguel Primo de Rivera, who staged a coup and took over the government - although he allowed Alfonso to stay on as figurehead.

General Primo, a jovial, hard-drinking man, was quite kindly as military dictators go. He built roads and made the trains run on time. But time was against him. By 1930 he'd lost the support of his fellow generals and had to resign

Swings and roundabouts

By 1930 when Primo resigned, most people had had enough of incompetent kings and military dictatorships. In elections the following year, Spain chose a liberal, republican government. King Alfonso, still the nominal head of state, left the country at last and the 'Second Republic' was born.

The new republican government was in a hurry to modernise things. Three thousand new schools were built, then seven thousand more. Priests, monks and nuns were barred from teaching. Divorce by consent was legalised. Women got the right to vote.

Giving the vote to women was a dangerous thing to do at that time. Women were more traditional than men and more likely to listen to the sermons of the anti-liberal bishops. In fresh elections in 1933, the women's vote helped oust the liberals from power. A right-wing government was voted in which set out to overturn everything the last one had started.

THIS WAY TO THE POLLING BOOTH, LADIES.

But then - in yet another swing of the pendulum - the left-wing and the liberals banded together to form a 'Popular Front'. The Popular Front swept to power in fresh elections in 1936. Left-wingers in the new government, every bit as uncompromising as the right-wingers, pushed for even more radical reforms.

The right-wingers sulked - bitterly.

The last coup
In 1936, most people wanted peace and quiet and to get on with their lives but extremists from both sides wouldn't let them. Strikes, killings and mob violence tore Spain apart. A report to the parliament on public unrest between February and March, when the Popular Front was in power, showed:

269 people assassinated	13 general strikes
1,287 people injured	251 churches set on fire
69 political offices destroyed	160 churches destroyed

It was a shambles. In the background, the generals did more than sulk - they plotted to seize power. Colonel Juan Blanco, called the 'Hyena of the Asturias', coordinated the plot and General Francisco Franco was chosen to lead it. Franco was forty-four years old, a good general and utterly ruthless. On 16 July 1936, the Spanish army in Morocco rose in revolt against the Second Republic, followed next day by soldiers on the mainland. On 19 July, Franco flew to Morocco where he took command of the rebellion.

The Civil War had started.

In Brief - 1900-1936	
1909	Anarchist riots in Barcelona.
1921	General Primo seizes power.
1930	General Primo resigns.
	Alfonso XIII leaves the country.
	Start of the Second Republic.
1936	Start of the Civil War.

THE SPANISH CIVIL WAR
TO VISIT, OR NOT TO VISIT, THE VALLEY OF THE FALLEN

God on our side

Franco led his men across the Strait of Gibraltar to Spain in late July 1936. As his ships set sail, it was said that the Virgin Mary appeared before them to show the way - Nationalists liked to portray their rebellion as a holy war against heathen anarchists and communists rather than as what it really was - a military rebellion against an elected government.

If you're near Coruña

Francisco Franco was born in Ferrol, a port on the Galician coast just north of Coruña. The family house was Calle Maria 136. Until recently the town square was dominated by his statue, but it was repeatedly splattered in paint and eggs by ill-wishers. It's been moved to the naval dockyard for safekeeping.

A hillside in Granada

By August 1936, the Spanish Civil War was raging across an unhappy country. That month, Federico Garcia Lorca, a thirty-seven-year-old poet, was taken from prison in Granada where he'd been held for two days without charge. He was bundled into a car and driven into the hills outside the town. There in the sweltering night, he was forced to dig his own grave. Then he was shot.

Lorca is reckoned to be the greatest Spanish poet of the twentieth century. He was already famous when he died but his fame gave him no protection. He was shot by 'Nationalists' because he was gay and a liberal. His murderers were most likely members of either the Civil Guard or of the Falange, the Spanish fascist movement, or perhaps of both.

Civil Guard

The Guardia Civil *was formed in 1844 to police rural areas and put down brigands. An elite group, it was always right wing. In the Civil War it took more casualties than any other Nationalist force. The standard uniform was green with a distinctive, patent-leather, tricorn hat. In 1928, Garcia Lorca had written a poem,* The Ballad of the Civil Guard, *in which he described the guardsmen as having their skulls cast in lead and their souls made of patent leather, which can't have endeared him to them.*

The Spanish Civil War was just a month old when Lorca was killed. It had nearly three more years to run (16 July 1936 - 28 March 1939). In it, the hatreds nursed so long and so fondly by both liberals and traditionalists erupted like a horrible, festering sore. Lorca's death was one in over half a million on both sides.

The bullring at Badajoz

The Republicans fought as best they could. All across Spain, Republican supporters in suits, dungarees and working clothes of all kinds drilled in parks and plazas. But they were at a severe disadvantage. Most of the regular army sided with with the Nationalists.

Both sides committed atrocities during the Civil War. Republicans burned churches and killed fascist prisoners; Nationalists shot prisoners and political opponents. However, Republican atrocities were never the result of orders from high up whereas the Nationalists used terror to crush their opponents as deliberate policy. In this 'holy war', as they saw their uprising, anything was justified. Throughout the conflict, large numbers of Republicans were shot in 'reprisals'. The massacre of Badajoz was typical. Nationalists took the town in August 1936 shortly after the war started, after ferocious hand-to-hand fighting in which two Republicans were slaughtered on the steps of the high altar.

When it was over, the Nationalists herded 1,800 of the Republican defenders into the Badajoz bullring and shot them in cold blood. Eye witnesses described the blood as flowing 'palm deep' across the road outside.

The Alcázar of Toledo

At the start of the Civil War, in July 1936, Nationalist soldiers and members of the National Guard in Toledo were outnumbered by the townspeople who were mostly Republican sympathisers. The Nationalists took refuge in the Alcázar, the ancient Almohad fortress, taking the wives and children of leading Republicans with them as hostages. Republican forces besieged the Alcázar and the siege lasted for months and was very bitter. The defenders were reduced to eating rats.

In September, Franco's army came to the relief of the defenders. There was no sign of the hostages.

As for the anarchists, they fought bravely but military discipline is hardly an anarchist virtue. At the height of the conflict, when they were besieged in Barcelona, there were reports of anarchist battalions leaving the front line in order to vote on what to do next. By October

1936, Franco had set up an alternative government in Burgos, in Old Castile in the north. By November he was at the outskirts of Madrid.

Gernika

The Spanish Civil War was the Second World War in miniature and it finished just before the Second World War started. It was the same fight writ small, like a rehearsal for the main event - democracy on one side, fascism on the other. German and Italian fascists supported the Nationalists. British and French democrats supported the Republicans - together with not-so-democratic Russian communists.

For the Nationalists
Fascist Italy and Germany sent troops, tanks and planes.

For the Republicans
The Republicans were handicapped because western democracies such as France, Britain and America chose to stay neutral, but individual socialists and communists from Britain and other countries joined 'International Brigades' and set sail for Spain, about 55,000 men in total. Also, Communist Russia sent weapons to the Spanish communists, hoping to turn Spain into a communist state later.

Without German artillery and planes, the Nationalists might not have won the Civil War. The German Nazis were very useful. Their Condor Legion of four bomber squadrons and four fighter squadrons was set up specially to help Franco.

Despite having the military advantage the Nationalist advance was quite slow. In the spring of 1937, they were held up in the Basque country by dogged resistance from local Republicans. At this point, the Nationalist leadership decided that the people must be terrorised into surrender. At their request, on Monday 26 April 1937, the German Condor Legion bombed the ancient Basque city of Gernika from the air. Monday happened to be market day and the town was full of people from the surrounding countryside. Those who survived the three-hour bombing were then machine-gunned by the German fighter planes.

The painter Pablo Picasso, who was Spanish and a communist, recorded the atrocity in a painting called simply *Gernika*. Gernika is famous because of this painting and because it was the first time in history that bombers had annihilated a civilian target.

The Tree of Gernika
Gernika was chosen for destruction because it was the traditional meeting place of the Basque parliament. New rulers would meet with the Basque nobles under the Tree of Gernika, an oak tree. The tree was badly damaged by the German bombs, but its stump remains and is now protected by a neoclassical gazebo. It's in the gardens of the Casa de Juntas, the seat of the provincial government.

The Siege of Madrid

By 1938, it was obvious that the Republicans were going to lose the war. The International Brigades left Barcelona that October. There wasn't enough food for all the refugees in the city, let alone for its foreign defenders. The Barcelonans gave them a grateful send-off and prepared for a last stand - and for the inevitable mass executions by Nationalists after the city finally fell.

Barcelona fell in January 1939. Meanwhile the Republican government held its last meeting at Figueras near the French border and on 6 February 1939, Manuel Azaña, the last president of the Second Republic, went into exile along with half a million Republican soldiers and refugees.

Of the cities which mattered, only Madrid still held out against the Nationalists. It had been under siege since the very start of the war, but despite endless bombardments, attacks and counter-attacks, its defenders had held out. It had become a sort of mini workers' state. Luxury hotels and restaurants had been taken over, the rich were careful not to wear their best clothes and Nationalists lived in fear of discovery. When Nationalist forces finally entered the city, on 27 March 1939, the dirty, exhausted defenders knew all too well what was in store for them.

The fall of Madrid was the last act of the Civil War. After that, all the Nationalists had to do was to mop up a final few pockets of resistance. The Pope sent Franco a message of congratulation.

If you're visiting the Escorial

Franco's Folly

More than half a million people died in the Civil War. Of these, over 100,000 were executed by Nationalist forces during the conflict and about 28,000 afterwards. General Franco was vindictive in his hour of victory.

After it was over, the Nationalists held about two million Republicans in concentration camps and prisons around the country. These prisoners were a useful source of cheap labour. Fifty miles northwest of Madrid, not far from the Palace of the Escorial, you can visit the Valley of the Fallen, Franco's monument to the war, otherwise known as 'Franco's Folly'. It's a vast basilica carved out of the granite hillside by Republican prisoners. They had to work round the clock so as to finish on schedule. Outside, a huge, concrete cross towers above the hills. Inside, piped music fills the dank, cold air. It's a spooky place. Between fifteen and twenty thousand corpses from both sides lie buried behind the walls and tapestries. Franco and José Antonio Primo de Rivera, founder of the Falange, lie there too.

In Brief - The Civil War

16 February 1936	Left-wing Popular Front elected.
17 July 1936	Start of military uprising.
1 October 1936	Franco sets up separate, Nationalist government in Burgos.
November 1936	Start of the seige of Madrid.
26 April 1937	Nazis bomb Gernika.
1937-38	War of attrition.
December 1938	Nationalists advance on Catalonia.
5 March 1939	Republican government flees to France.
28 March 1939	Nationalists enter Madrid.

SUN AND SANGRIA

ALICANTE COMES INTO ITS OWN

What to do on the Costa del Sol

You're on the beach. You've nearly finished this book, which is possibly smeared with suntan oil and the remains of your ham sandwich. Now that you have a better knowledge of Spanish history, you may wish to put down your glass of sangria, if you've got one, and make a run for it - before you're crushed by Carthaginian elephants, imprisoned by the Inquisition, murdered by Moorish mercenaries or nobbled by Nationalist soldiers. At least you're near the water if they want to bury you below the high tide mark.

Relax! You're safe, except from the effects of sunburn, booze and overeating. There are no fascists lurking round corners, no Inquisition, no foreign domination. How come, after such a long and in many ways tragic history, Spain has become this magically prosperous and tolerant country?

If you're a tourist, you're part of the reason.

Franco was smarter than other fascist dictators of the 1930s. He stayed out of the Second World War, much to Hitler's disappointment. As a result, his regime lasted right up to 1975. For more than thirty years, while the rest of western Europe surged forward, Spain had to endure his repressive, backward-looking government.

But although Franco was extremely repressive, he imposed order - and he encouraged tourism. He was wise enough to see that, although Spain had little in the way of modern industry at that time, it had sunshine and sandy beaches in abundance. Sunshine and sand which could be converted into money. He encouraged hotel building along the Costa Brava, the Costa Blanca and the Costa del Sol. Through the 60s and 70s, mass tourism together with money from Spaniards working abroad, fuelled the Spanish economy. Spain began to prosper. On the back of tourism, other industries began to flourish as well.

Goodbye Franco
Franco lived into his eighties. By the end he was a tiny (he was only five foot three in his prime), semi-senile old man. He finally resigned in 1973 but lived on for two more years while an interim Prime Minister held the reins. By then he'd groomed Juan Carlos, grandson of Alfonso XIII, to take over the government. Franco confidently expected Juan to continue the Francoist system of dictatorship.

Franco died in November 1975 and Juan Carlos took up his crown and became head of state. He immediately pardoned a large number of political prisoners. Franco must have turned in his coffin, recently installed in the basilica of the Valley of the Fallen. And that was only the beginning.

Juan Carlos turned out to be one of the best kings Spain has ever had. He moved fast to demolish the remains of the Franco regime, being clever enough and careful enough not to enrage too many elderly Francoist generals while he went about it.

In Brief - the End of Franco's Dictatorship	
1976	The Spanish Sahara, Spain's last attempted colony, given up.
1 April 1977	National Movement (Franco's political base) abolished.
28 April 1977	Free trades unions allowed.
15 June 1977	General Election.
1978	Freely elected Cortes makes Spain a constitutional monarchy.

Separatists and terrorists

Franco retired two years before he died. His chosen replacement was Admiral Carrero Blanco, who was to run the country until Juan Carlos was ready to take over. Carrero was murdered by Basque terrorists in December 1973. Throughout the Franco years and beyond, Basque extremists of the ETA had been using terrorism to campaign for an independent Basque state.

Carrero Blanco was a man of regular habits. His assassins knew exactly where to find him. His car was always parked in exactly the same spot after morning mass, so they dug a tunnel under the street and buried a sack-load of high explosives below his parking spot. They took their time, posing as artists and sculptors while they drilled and dug. On the appointed day, a massive explosion blew the admiral's car with him inside clean over a five-storey building. He was dead before he hit the ground.

ETA stands for *Euskadi Ta Askatasuna*, which means '*Euskadi* (the Basque language) and Liberty'. Originally the group called themselves ATA, which stands for *Aberri Ta Askatasuna*, meaning 'Homeland and Liberty', but then it was pointed out that *Ata* means duck in one of the many Basque dialects so they had to change it.

The Basque terrorists are an unpopular and tiny minority, but they're just the extreme end of a widespread dislike of the central government common to most of the Spanish regions. The government in Madrid tries to cater for this regional pride. As part of the constitution of 1978, Spain was divided into seventeen autonomous regions, including the Basque country and Catalonia.

Nowadays, many Basques and Catalonians still seek full independence, but they're peaceful about it and want nothing to do with the terrorists. Regional nationalism mostly focuses on the use of the regional languages. Local spellings have become part of the quest for regional identity. They're harmless, but they do make road signs difficult for tourists.

The last squeak

Not so very long ago, a great many Spaniards still thought that isolation was a good thing. They actually *liked* being cut off from Europe. A nineteenth-century senator, Señor González Castejón, summed up their attitude:

> *In my opinion, the Pyrenees should never be levelled, not for any reason, ever. On the contrary, another whole range of mountains, placed on top of the mountains we now have, would be even more to our advantage.*

117

Senor Castejón would be disappointed by how things have turned out. To all intents and purposes the Pyrenees have ceased to exist - or at least they've been considerably flattened. And most modern Spaniards welcome the change.

Most, but not all, in February 1981, diehard supporters of the old Francoist regime had one more try for power. Lieutenant Colonel Antonio Tejero led a troop of Civil Guard soldiers into the Chamber of Deputies. The soldiers fired their machine guns in the air and ordered the deputies present to lie on the floor. Meanwhile other rebels seized the Madrid television station. The deputies were held hostage for eighteen hours while the rebels desperately broadcast messages asking other soldiers to join in. The revolt fizzled, despite all their pleas for support. This was because King Juan Carlos spoke out against it on national television as soon as he got the chance.

The attempted coup by Colonel Antonio Tejero was the last squeak of the Francoists. As Tejero found out to his cost, Spain had no wish to go back to the bad old days. Spanish people wanted an open and generous society. In 1986, Spain joined the European Community. In 1992 she hosted the Olympic Games in Barcelona. Since then, progress has continued.

For better or worse, and in Spain's case it's definitely for better, Spain is now a fully paid-up member of the modern world.

Long may it continue.

THE RULERS OF SPAIN FROM 1516
(with the rulers of Castile and León from 1035)

Castile and León
1065-72	Ferdinand I (León 1037-65)
1065-72	Sancho II (Castile only)
1072-1109	Alfonso VI (León 1065-1109)
1109-26	Urraca
1126-57	Alfonso VII
1157-58	Sancho III (Castile only)
1157-88	Ferdinand II (León only)
1158-1214	Alfonso VIII (Castile only)
1188-1230	Alfonso IX (León only)
1214-17	Henry I (Castile only)
1217-52	Ferdinand III (León 1230-52)
1252-84	Alfonso X
1284-95	Sancho IV
1295-1312	Ferdinand IV
1312-50	Alfonso XI
1350-69	Peter the Cruel
1369-79	Henry II of Trastamara
1379-90	John I
1390-1406	Henry III
1406-54	John II
1454-1474	Henry IV
1474-1504	Isabella I (married to Ferdinand II, ruler of Aragon 1479-1516)
1504-06	Joanna the Mad (Habsburg)
1506	Phillip I, the Handsome
1506 - 1516	Ferdinand II (regent for Joanna the Mad)

Unified 'Spain' - Habsburg Dynasty
1516-56	Charles I (Emperor Charles V)
1556-98	Philip II
1598-1621	Philip III
1621-65	Philip IV
1665-1700	Charles II

Bourbon Dynasty

1700-24	Philip V
1724	Louis I
1724-46	Philip V (again)
1746-59	Ferdinand VI
1759-88	Charles III
1788-1808	Charles IV
1808	Ferdinand VII

French Occupation

1808-13	Joseph Bonaparte

Bourbon Dynasty

1814-33	Ferdinand VII (again)
1833-70	Isabella II (in exile 1868-70)

General Prim and Amadeo

1868-70	General Juan Prim
1870-73	Amadeo of Savoy

First Republic

1873-74	various presidents

Bourbon Dynasty

1874-85	Alfonso XII
1886-1931	Alfonso XIII

Second Republic (presidents)

1931-36	Niceto Alcala Zamora
1936-39	Manuel Azaña

Dictatorship

1939-75	General Francisco Franco

Bourbon Dynasty

1975 -	Juan Carlos I

Important Dates

BC

*c.*20-12,000	Stone Age cave painters of Altamira and elsewhere.
*c.*3-2,000	Iberians arrive from North Africa, metals are worked for the first time.
*c.*1,100	Phoenicians found Cádiz and other cities and trade for silver.
*c.*900	Celts begin to arrive in northern Spain bringing knowledge of iron with them.
*c.*600	Greeks establish Alicante, Empuriés and other cities on the east coast.
237	Carthaginians invade southern Spain and build Cartagena.
218-201	Romans defeat the Carthaginians.
218 - AD409	Spain is part of the Roman Empire.

AD

*c.*100-200	Christianity spreads from the south.
409	Vandals and other barbarian tribes invade Roman Spain.
414	Visigoths arrive and kick the Vandals into North Africa.
589	Visigoths become Roman Catholics and Catholicism becomes the official religion of the country.
711	Muslims invade from Morocco and defeat Roderic the Visigothic king.
*c.*722	Pelayo defeats a Muslim army in the vale of Covadonga and founds the tiny Christian kingdom of Asturias in the north - the start of the *Reconquista*.
756-1010	Córdoba dominates Muslim Spain.

801	Frankish troops of the Emperor Charlemagne found what will later become Catalonia.
899	Bones of Saint James the Apostle discovered at Santiago de Compostela.
929	Caliphate of Córdoba declared independent of Baghdad.
997	Al Mansur attacks Compostela.
1000-35	Kingdoms of Castile and Aragón are founded.
1010-1248	Seville is the most powerful Muslim state.
1085	Alfonso VI of Castile captures Toledo.
1086	Almoravids from Morocco come to the aid of the Spanish Muslims and conquer Andalusia.
1094	El Cid captures Valencia.
1137	Aragón and Catalonia are united.
1145	Almohads invade Andalusia from Morocco.
1212	Christians defeat the Muslims at the battle of Las Navas de Tolosa.
1230	Castile and Leon are united.
1236	Ferdinand III captures Córdoba.
1248	Ferdinand III captures Seville.
1248-1492	Granada is the most important Muslim state.
1469	Marriage of Ferdinand of Aragón and Isabella of Castile unites most of Christian Spain.
1478	Inquisition founded by Isabella.
1492	Ferdinand and Isabella capture Granada - the *Reconquista* is complete.
1492	The Jews are expelled from Spain.
1492	Columbus discovers the Bahamas and

	claims his discovery for Ferdinand and Isabella thus paving the way for the Spanish Empire in the Americas.
1502	Muslims in Spain must either convert to Christianity or leave. Most choose to convert and are called *Moriscos.*
1516-56	Reign of Charles I, first of the Hapsburgs.
1556-98	Reign of Philip II
1561	Madrid becomes the capital of Spain.
1584	Palace of the Escorial completed.
1568	Start of the Dutch War of Independence.
1588	England defeats the Invincible Armada.
1605	First part of Don Quixote is published.
1609	Philip III expels the *Moriscos* (Muslim converts to Christianity) from Spain.
1621-65	Reign of Philip IV. Start of the long decline.
1700-46	Reign of Philip V, the first Bourbon.
1701-15	War of the Spanish Succession.
1704	Treaty of Utrecht. Gibraltar signed over to the British.
1759-88	Reign of Charles III.
1808	Invasion of revolutionary French forces. Joseph Bonaparte becomes king.
1810-26	Spanish colonies in America move towards complete independence.
1812	Cortes of Cádiz establishes a liberal constitution.
1814-33	Reign of Ferdinand VII.
1834	Inquisition abolished.
1873-74	First Republic.
1875-85	Reign of Alfonso XII.
1898	Spanish-American War. Spain loses her last major colonies.

1902-31	Alfonso XIII reigns but fails to rule.
1914-18	Spain remains neutral during the First World War.
1923-30	Dictatorship of General Primo de Rivera.
1931-36	Second Republic.
1936	Popular Front wins power in a general election. This is followed by a short period of near anarchy.
1936-39	Spanish Civil War.
1939-	Spain remains neutral during the Second World War.
1939-75	Dictatorship of General Francisco Franco.
1975	Juan Carlos becomes king.
1977	First general election since 1936.

Index

Jews 9,19,20,27,30,34,49,53,
70-74,89
Juan Carlos, King 115,116,
118
Juana 'la Loca' 59,70
Julian, Count 24,25

Kolaios 16,17

Las Navas de Tolosa 34
León 30,39-41
Leovigild 24
Lepanto, Battle of 66
limpieza de sangre 74-75
Linajudos 74
Lope de Vega 65,66
Lorca, Federico Garcia
106-108
Louis XIV 84

Madrid 21,47,61-63,67,69,82,
85,88,92,93,110,112,117,
118
Maimonides, Moses 34
Majorca 58
Malaga 16,22
Manzanares, River 79
Marcus Aurelius 19
Maria Luisa, Queen 92
Marranos 72,73
Martial 19
Mary Tudor 64
matadors 89-91
Medellin 56
Medina Azahara 28
Medina Sidonia, Duke of 65
Mérida 20,21
Mesta 50,78,85
Mexico 54-56,97
Minorca 58
Mohammed V 35

Moriscos 72-74
Mozárabes 30,34,63
Mudéjars 42,63
Murillo, Bartolomé 95
Muslims 5,7,9,25-39,42,45-50,
52,53,63,71-76,89

Napoleon Bonaparte 92,93,95,
97
National Movement 116
Navarre 40,41,44,58
Nero 19,21

Pelayo 38-40
Peninsular War 94
Peru 56,57
Peter the Cruel 72
Philip I, the Handsome 59
Philip II 60-66,70
Philip III 60
Philip IV 60,80
Philip V 83,84
Phoenicians 12,16-18
Picasso, Pablo 111
Pilgrim Way 44,45
Pizarro, Francisco 57
Plateresque 63
Popular Front 104,105,113
Portugal 10,21,41,46,51,52,54
Prim, General Juan 99-101
Primo de Rivera, José 113
Primo de Rivera, Miguel 103,
104,106
Protestants 63,64,70-72,85,
102
Puente Viesgo 14
Pyrenees 10,84,117,118

Reccared 24
Reconquista 12,38-50,53,57,
66,70